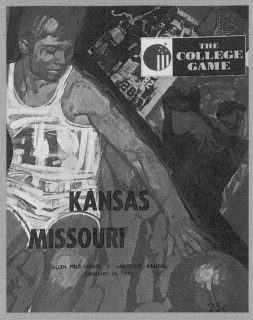

THE COLLEGE GAME

KANSAS
MISSOURI

ALLEN FIELD HOUSE • LAWRENCE, KANSAS
FEBRUARY 20, 1972

25c

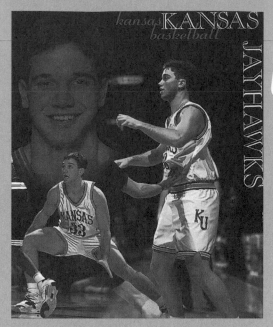

kansas KANSAS
basketball
JAYHAWKS

KANSAS
KU

University of
KANSAS
VS.
UTAH STATE

Wednesday, December 6, 1950

Hoch Auditorium
Lawrence

Next Home Game
SPRINGFIELD
December 19

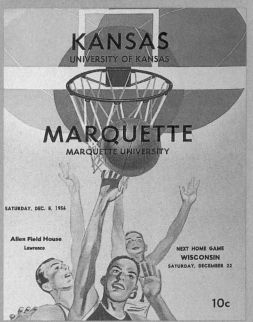

KANSAS
UNIVERSITY OF KANSAS

MARQUETTE
MARQUETTE UNIVERSITY

SATURDAY, DEC. 8, 1956

Allen Field House
Lawrence

NEXT HOME GAME
WISCONSIN
SATURDAY, DECEMBER 22

10c

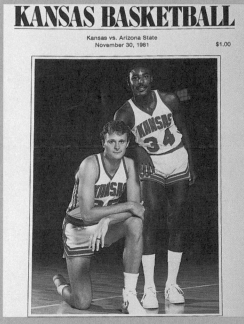

KANSAS BASKETBALL

Kansas vs. Arizona State
November 30, 1981 $1.00

KANSAS 34

OFFICIAL SOUVENIR PROGRAM

KANSAS
OKLAHOMA

MONDAY
FEBRUARY 19, 1962

ALLEN FIELD HOUSE
LAWRENCE

LAST HOME GAME
OKLA. STATE

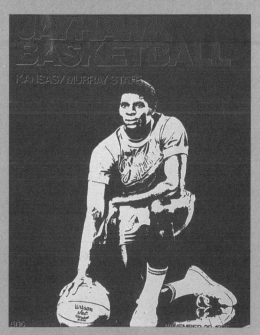

JAYHAWK
BASKETBALL
KANSAS/MURRAY STATE

Kansas / Oklahoma / February 5, 1977 / 50c

Kansas:
The Basketball School

s Ackerman • I.R. Adams • Jerry Alberts • Bob Allen • Dr. Forrest C. "Phog"
en • Harry Allen • John Anderson • NCAA Champions 1952 • Wilfred Belgard
m Bishop • Charlie Black • Charlie Black • C.J. Bliss • Rodger Bohnenstiehl
H. Born • Bill Bridges • Roger Brown • John Buescher • John Bunn • Glenn
rton • NCAA Runner up 1940 • Wilt Chamberlain • Lawrence Cole • Norm
ok • Lyman Corlis • Al Correll • Forrest "Frosty" Cox • NCAA Third Place
42 • Dallas Dobbs • Don Dousman • Ralph "Stuffy" Dunmire • NCAA Runner
1953 • Don Ebling • Ray Ebling • Nolen Ellison • Gene Elstun • Paul Endacott
Howard Engelman • Ray Evans • NCAA Runner up 1957 • Ren Frana • Jerry
rdner • Harry Gibson • Gale Gordon • Dale Greenlee • C.R. Greenlees • NIT
nner up 1968 • W.O. Hamilton • Dick Harp • Paul Harrington • Bob Helzer
ayne Hightower • James Hill • Charlie Hoag • Claude Houchin • Bill Hougland
P. Hunter • NCAA Fourth Place 1971 • Bill Johnson • Lew Johnson • Tommy
hnson • Wes Johnson • NCAA Fourth Place 1974 • Francis Kappelman • John
ller • Al Kelley • Dean Kelley • Bob Kenney • Dee Ketchum • Maurice King
m Kivisto • John Kline • Danny Knight • Missouri Valley Champions 13 times
et Lawrence • Delvy Lewis • Bill Lienhard • Riley Lochmann • Arthur "Dutch"
berg • Ron Loneski • Vern Long • Al Lopes • Wayne Louderback • Clyde
rellette • Big Six Champions 12 times • Kelsey Matthews • George Mc Cune
rold McSpadden • M.B. Miller • Ralph Miller • Roger Morningstar • Bob Mosby
Seven Champion 5 times • Dr. James Naismith • Aubrey Nash • Lawrence
son • Dean Nesmith • Ray Noble • Big Eight Champion 6 times • Ted O'Leary
d Owens • Herbert Owens • Ted Owens • 23 All Americans • Lee Page
n Parker • Harold Patterson • Al Peterson • Fred Pralle • Ernie Quigley
ympians • Gordon Reynolds • Dave Robisch • George Rody • Paul Rogers
lph Rupp • Pierre Russell • 60 All Conference Selections • Bill Sapp • Dave
ichtle • Karl Schlademan • Harold Schmidt • Otto Schnellbacher • Kirk
tt • Bruce Sloan • C.A. Smith • Dean Smith • Ephraim Sorenson • Ralph "Lefty"
oull • Bud Stallworth • George Stuckey • Rick Suttle • Will Sutton • Big Eight
urnament Champion 11 times • Dave Taynor • Russell Thomson • Ernie Unfraub

Kansas
Kansas St.
souvenir program

KANSAS 34
KU

jayhawk

THE KANSAS CENTURY

THE KANSAS CENTURY

100 HUNDRED YEARS
OF CHAMPIONSHIP
JAYHAWK BASKETBALL

DAVID HALBERSTAM
TED O'LEARY
BILL MAYER
JOE POSNANSKI
CHUCK WOODLING
JOHN MCLENDON
ALEXANDER WOLFF

CONTENTS

STAFF FOR THIS BOOK

Editor:
RICH CLARKSON

Editorial Assistant
AARON BRINKMAN

Art Director:
KATE GLASSNER BRAINERD

For the University of Kansas
DOUG VANCE, DEAN BUCHAN

Production Coordinator
EMMETT JORDAN

www.andrewsmcmeel.com

ISBN: 0-8362-5303-5
LIBRARY OF CONGRESS CATOLOGING-IN-PUBLICATION DATA ON FILE

It was a glorious day when Allen Fieldhouse was finally dedicated. Dr. Allen spoke during the halftime program as Chancellor Franklin D. Murphy awaited his turn. The Board of Regents and Governor Ed Arn shared the floor during a salute to past basketball greats.

100 YEARS

KANSAS BASKETBALL, THEN AND NOW

1898

Dr. James Naismith, the inventor of the game and a health and physical education instructor at Kansas, coaches KU's first basketball team. Naismith's team loses its first game but finishes the year 7-4.

1907

Forrest Allen, who played for Naismith, begins a long and storied career as KU's head coach at the tender age of 22. Allen goes against the early advice of Naismith who said, "You don't coach basketball Forrest, you just play it." Later, Naismith recognizes Allen's abilities and labels him "the father of basketball coaching." Allen coaches 39 years at Kansas, winning 590 games.

1922

With future Hall of Fame member Paul Endacott leading the way, Kansas finishes 16-2, ties for the Missouri Valley Conference title, and is crowned national champion by the Helms Foundation.

1923

Behind Endacott, Tus Ackerman and Charlie Black, KU wins the Missouri Valley title outright, finishing 17-1 and again claiming the Helms Foundation national title.

1930

Kansas graduate Adolph Rupp, who played on the national championship teams of 1922 and 1923, begins his illustrious head coaching career at Kentucky.

1939

Naismith dies Nov. 28 in Lawrence and is buried in Memorial Park Cemetery. World War II delays the start of construction of the Naismith Hall of Fame.

1940

In the second year of the new NCAA national championship, Kansas plays Indiana for the title with a team lead by future Hall of Fame player Ralph Miller, Bob Allen (son of the coach), Howard Engleman and future KU coach Dick Harp. Kansas loses to the Hoosiers 60-42 in Kansas City's new Municipal Auditorium.

1952

Kansas is the most dominant team in college basketball, capturing the NCAA tournament and finishing 28-3. Future Hall of Famer Clyde Lovellette leads the nation in scoring (28.6 points per game) and puts up 33 points in the championship game against St. John's. Seven members of that team and Dr. Allen are members of the U.S. Olympic basketball team, winning the gold medal in Helsinki.

1955

Allen Fieldhouse opens its doors on March 1 to a crowd of 17,228 that watches Kansas beat Kansas State, 77-66, beginning a new era in Jayhawk basketball. The next fall, in Phog Allen's last year as head coach, freshman Wilt Chamberlain leads the frosh team past the varsity.

1956

In his first varsity game, Chamberlain scores 52 points in the season-opening game Dec. 3 against Northwestern.

1957

Chamberlain is the dominant player in college basketball, averaging 29.6 points per game. He leads Dick Harp's team to the NCAA title game where the Jayhawks lose a in triple-overtime to North Carolina.

1968

The Naismith Memorial Basketball Hall of Fame opens in Springfield, Mass. Under head coach Ted Owens, KU claws its way to the NIT finals before losing to Dayton.

1969

Kansas defeats Colorado February 1, enabling Owens to celebrate the Jayhawks' 1,000th basketball victory.

1971

Dave Robisch and Bud Stallworth lead Kansas to a 14-0 Big Eight Conference record and a trip to the Final Four.

1972

Playing against Missouri Feb. 26, Bud Stallworth erupts for 50 points, setting a KU scoring record for a conference game, a mark that still stands.

1974

A Jayhawk team with no superstar finishes 13-1 in the Big Eight and earns another trip to the Final Four, losing to Marquette in the semifinals.

1978

Led by freshman point guard Darnell Valentine, the Jayhawks win the Big Eight crown with a 13-1 mark and finish ranked in the nation's top 10 teams.

1986

Larry Brown puts together one of KU's most talented teams: Behind Danny Manning, Calvin Thompson, Ron Kellogg, Greg Dreiling and Cedric Hunter, KU wins a school record 35 games and goes to the Final Four in Dallas.

1988

Cinderella Kansas wins its first NCAA title in 36 years when Danny (Manning) and the Miracles overcome much adversity and long odds to beat Oklahoma 83-79 for the 50th NCAA title in Kansas City's Kemper

Arena. Manning, the consensus national player of the year, scores 33 points and pulls down 18 rebounds in the title game.

In May, KU graduate and then-Oregon State coach Ralph Miller becomes the 13th KU inductee into the Basketball Hall of Fame. In July, Roy Williams becomes just the seventh coach in Kansas basketball history.

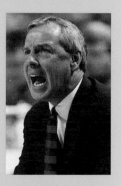

1991

Unranked in some preseason polls, KU puts together an NCAA run with wins over No. 3 Indiana, No. 2 Arkansas and No. 4 North Carolina. The Jayhawks lose to Duke in the NCAA title game in Indianapolis.

1993

Williams leads Kansas to its second Final Four in three years and its third consecutive Big Eight championship. Led by the senior guard duo of Rex Walters and Adonis Jordan, the Jayhawks

win the NCAA Midwest Regional to earn a trip to New Orleans for the NCAA Finals, where they lose to North Carolina in the semifinals.

1997

Ranked No. 1 in the nation for virtually the entire season, the Jayhawks lose only one game, that at Missouri, but return to win the first Big 12 title as well as the Big 12 Postseason Tournament.

But they are surprised by the eventual national champion, Arizona, in the upset game of the year.

All eyes in Allen Fieldhouse
watched Nick Bradford score while
driving the baseline as KU defeated
Iowa State in a Big 12 matchup
early in the 1996-97 season.

MEMORABLE MOMENTS

Over 99 years, basketballs have been lofted to the hoop by nearly 2,000 athletes wearing the crimson and blue. Seven serious and dedicated men have yelled advice from the sidelines, and hundreds of thousands of Kansans have shrieked their delight or disdain. Here are some memorable moments, individuals and images.

The game of basketball — and its inventor, Dr. James Naismith — have held the attention of thousands of boys. Perched on the west steps of Robinson Gymnasium, the three grandsons of Naismith listened to the physical education professor talk about this most American of all games. Today, Kansas coach Roy Williams (above) pays his respects during his daily run past the Naismith grave in east Lawrence's Memorial Park Cemetery.

Allen Fieldhouse, the premier arena of the college game, honors the father of basketball coaching. The game was passed from Naismith to Forrest C. "Phog" Allen, who virtually invented the art of coaching basketball, something Naismith once decried: "You don't coach basketball, you just play it." But as Naismith watched KU practice in the '30s, he saw another innovator at work and recanted his earlier words. After coaching at KU for 39 seasons, Dr. Allen posed in Allen Fieldhouse the afternoon before it was dedicated in his honor.

The most heralded athlete to play atop Mt. Oread changed the college game. Wilt Chamberlain
(right) arrived from Overbrook High School in Philadelphia amidst much conjecture as to what
Phog and the alumni had done to entice him to Lawrence. But when Wilt took the raised floor at

Allen Fieldhouse with newly promoted coach Dick Harp (left) presiding over the moment, The Stilt was the center of attention. And in his three eventful years at Kansas before turning pro with the Globetrotters, Chamberlain's performances left an unforgettable mark on the college game and KU.

The students are the sixth man of Kansas basketball. Although many schools have strong student support, KU students have nurtured traditions, emotions and pride in their basketball that are uniquely Jayhawk. Rallies to send off or to welcome home the team have always been part of the Kansas experience. This 1952 celebration (left) extended the tradition as students climbed atop Jimmy Green, spilled across Jayhawk Boulevard and leaned from the windows of old Frazier to welcome home KU's first NCAA national champions.

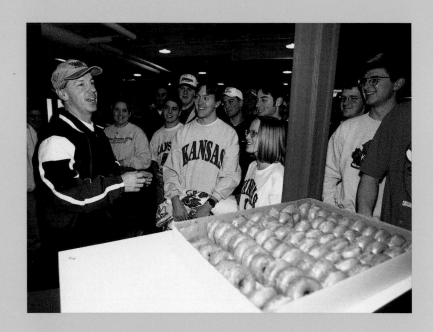

Today, some KU students arrive for the game two days early so they can claim the prime front-row seats. They bring sleeping bags, books and laptops, and friends hold places when class times interfere. Even coach Williams gets into the act (above) by passing out late-night pizza and dough-nuts for the campers. When game time finally arrives and the opponents are introduced, everyone fakes disinterest by pretending to read the *University Daily Kansan*. But when the Jayhawks take the court, students let the confetti fly and the decibel level soars.

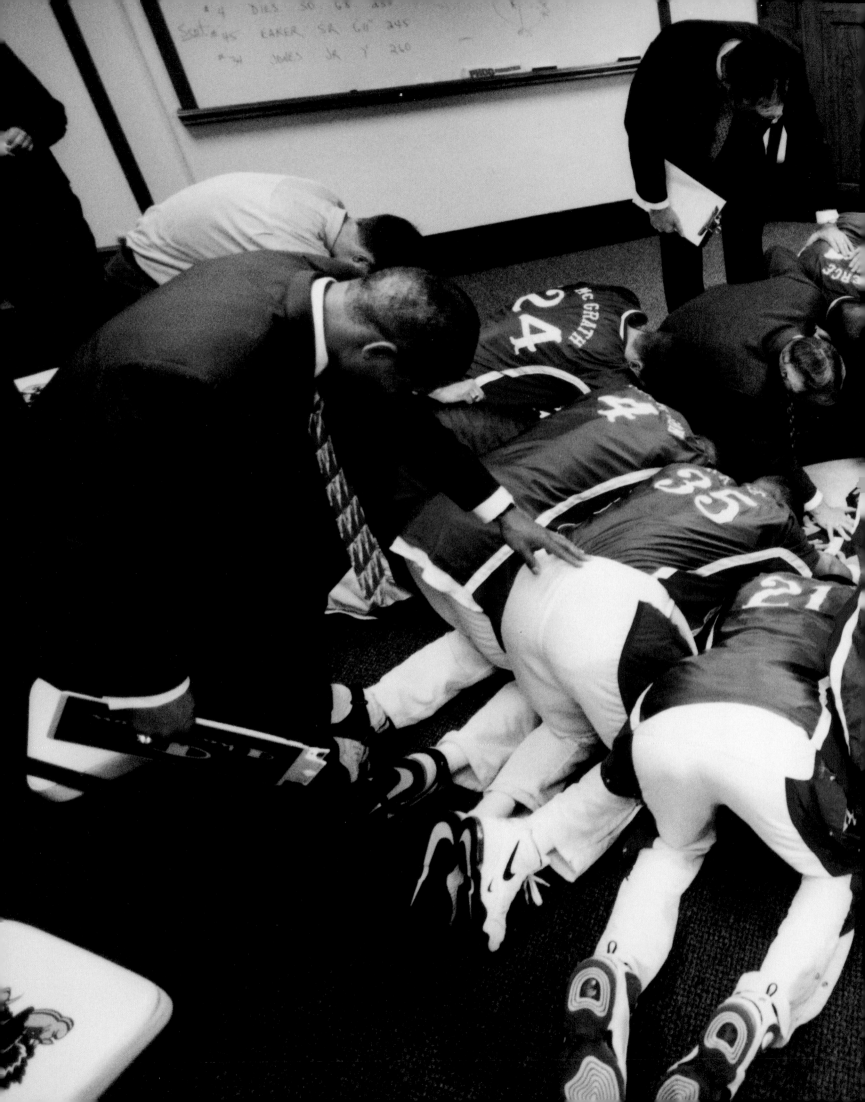

THE PASSION, THE INTENSITY, THE HISTORY

BY DAVID HALBERSTAM

A week before big games, hundreds of students, even though they already have general admission tickets, start lining up to get even better seats in Allen Fieldhouse. Roy Williams, the team's head coach, not unaware of the acoustical benefits that derive from this kind of passion, arrives at his office early in the morning and often hands out dozens of doughnuts to those in line. In the evening before he goes home he often stops by with slices of pizza. Passion, bordering on madness, is very much encouraged. The ticket itself is very simply the dearest in the state of Kansas and among the dearest in the Midwest. On occasion season tickets are passed on to the next generation in people's wills. When a local couple gets a divorce sometimes there is a bitter dispute over who gets custody of the tickets. Not surprisingly the passion and the noise generated in Lawrence are almost without parallel even in college basketball.

Winter, after all, in Kansas can be long and bleak, and, therefore, the light and energy and excitement found inside at a Jayhawk basketball game are singular. On those special nights when the team is at home, this arena becomes a universe all its own, a community within a community; a citadel of both adventure and pleasure, however momentary, in a region that does not offer many alternatives for several cold, hard months.

Rival coaches consider a visit to Allen Fieldhouse not unlike a visit to the hangman and with good reason: In the last 13 years the Jayhawks' home record is 178-14. And Kansas will open this forthcoming season with a run of 44 straight home victories. Inside the arena hangs a banner: "Pay Heed All Who Enter: BEWARE OF THE PHOG," a reference to Phog Allen, the formidable coach who essentially created basketball's preeminence here, and for whom the fieldhouse is named. Legend has it that in close games, the spirit of Phog Allen will enter the arena and cause a crucial turnover, or at the least slip inside the soul of a referee and help pressure him into a call against the visitors.

What we have here is not just sports, of course. What we have is theater disguised as basketball, where some 15 times a year, good takes on evil and almost always triumphs. Good, of course, is KU; Evil is Kansas State and Missouri and all the other unfortunate visitors whose somber, melancholy duty it is to play the role of the villain. Lawrence is a perfect venue for that: Allen Fieldhouse is both big-time and yet old-fashioned. It was one of the first of the modern basketball arenas, erected in 1956, but it was built to Allen's shrewd specifications, with the impact of the crowd very much in the mind of the by-then venerable coach. It is not like some of the more modern but rather genteel arenas, places where the best seats are somewhat removed from the action. Instead the fans are right down there in front as close to the action as possible; indeed, in any real sense they are a part of the action. In addition, unlike a lot of the newer basketball emporiums, the best seats do not go to the wealthiest (but occasionally slightly subdued) alumni, but to the students themselves. Phog wanted it that way and for a good reason: It may well be worth two or three home wins a year. No wonder then that Roy Williams, his lineal descendant, becomes for a few minutes a day a doughnut and pizza deliveryman.

IT IS NOT BY CHANCE THAT DR. JAMES NAISMITH WHO INVENTED THE SPORT WAS KANSAS'S FIRST COACH AND THAT HE IS BURIED HERE; AND THAT HIS SUCCESSOR AND PROTEGE WAS THE FABLED PHOG ALLEN.

This is a basketball school. Almost from the start, probably because of the force of Allen's personality, and his systematic success against historic rivals, Kansas became one of the rare big-time state universities in America where basketball was more important than football. Allen Fieldhouse was one of the first of the super arenas. If, in its sense of luxury and skyboxes it is a bit behind the contemporary curve, it was well ahead of that curve in the mid-'50s when it was completed. In that first year a season ticket for every home game cost all of $16, with free parking thrown in. A year later a freshman named Wilt Chamberlain arrived in Lawrence, and the athletic department, sensing that a big-time program was about to become even bigger, jacked the season ticket price up *four* dollars, an unheard of increase of 25 percent. There was a good deal of grumbling, but few people turned in their tickets, which was a good thing: Chamberlain played two full varsity seasons for Kansas. As a freshman he was not eligible for varsity play in that era, but in his first game at KU, his freshman team beat the Kansas varsity and in his first varsity game he scored 52 points.

Over the years the cost of the season ticket has gone up until today it costs $289 — with no parking thrown in. But given the madness it produces, it still remains something of a bargain. Contemporary Kansas basketball fever, of course, is nothing less than the proper legacy of an unusually rich history. For if the game as we know it was born in Springfield, Mass., then in any real sense the college game began here, and local aficionados take justifiable pride in thinking that this is the cradle of a sport that has now transfixed not just the nation but the rest of the world. It is not by chance that Dr. James Naismith who invented the sport was Kansas's first coach and that he is buried here; and that his successor and protege was the fabled Phog

Allen. Allen was not only the reigning coach of the early era, but he was the father of modern basketball coaching. It may be that Kansas basketball, located far from the dual media centers of America (New York and Los Angeles), does not quite get the national notoriety it deserves, but any visiting coach who has come here knows that Jayhawk teams are consistently among the best and toughest-minded in the country.

It is a long way from the time a century ago when its coach made about $2,000 a year and had several other major responsibilities to the sport, which because of the speed of its action, shares center stage with football in America today and whose professional players earn salaries in the tens of millions of dollars a year. Technically Naismith invented the game at a Springfield YMCA, using two peach baskets and hanging them at a height of 10 feet because that was the height of the available balcony he was using. Six years later, Naismith,

Dr. Naismith's first Kansas team went 7-4 in 1898-99. It would be only one of two winning seasons in Naismith's nine years as coach at KU.

OVER THE YEARS KANSAS HAS PRODUCED A PROTO-TYPE KIND OF TEAM, TOUGH, SMART, DISCIPLINED. TRADITION HAS TURNED INTO TRADEMARK.

more a man of God than of sport, was asked to come to the University of Kansas to teach and coach. His arrival was hardly an auspicious start for the birth of a big-time sport. The chancellor of the university, Francis Snow, had wanted a religious man more than a physical education man; among other things Snow wanted someone to lead all his students in prayer at the daily mandatory chapel sessions.

Naismith did not seem particularly passionate about the basketball job or the game that he had invented, least of all about winning with any regularity. He seemed to like the idea of hearty, youthful physical exertion as an end in itself. On occasion he would pull a player from a game and check his heartbeat, worried the player might be overexerting himself, not something that one expects to see Pat Riley or Phil Jackson doing these days. Naismith believed in a strong body and a clean life. He was a seriously religious man who turned down an endorsement from a cigarette company because he did not believe in tobacco. He drank, as far as his friends could tell, on only one occasion, when he wanted to check out alcohol's effect on athletic performance. He took drink after drink to measure what quickly became an obvious decline in his skills as a fencer.

Naismith handled the team's schedule, but he did not necessarily travel with his players. If he did travel, it was often to referee the game — things were, it seems, quite different then. Competition as the driving purpose in collegiate sport seems not to have interested him at all. No wonder then that he remains not merely the father of basketball but the only one of Kansas's coaches with a losing record. Later after retiring as coach, as Blair Kerkoff points out in his book on Phog Allen, Naismith would continue to attend KU games, where he would always sit in the same seat in the second row, ever impassive, showing neither pleasure nor passion, and never, apparently, cheering.

The real era of modern basketball began not with Naismith but his protege, Phog Allen. From the start Allen wanted more than to upgrade the physical condition of his young players — he wanted to win. He began coaching at Kansas in 1907 at the grand age of 22 years and five months old, which as fans here point out means that he still remains the youngest head coach in NCAA Division 1 history. Though he briefly left Kansas to coach elsewhere, he returned, and in the end he recorded 590 wins and 219 defeats. Over the years Allen became recognized as the game's foremost coach, and in time his progeny took his gospel and spread it throughout the country. Slowly and steadily under his tutelage a formidable basketball tradition was created here; other young men who believed they wanted to play — or to play and perhaps one day coach — began to arrive. In the days before big-time recruiting, Allen on his own had helped create a dynamic that drew young men to Lawrence. He became in time the progenitor of a long line of other prominent coaches, including Adolph Rupp of Kentucky, Dean Smith of North Carolina, and Ralph Miller of Oregon State. That means that among his contemporary lineal descendants in the family tree of coaching are Pat Riley, who played at Kentucky, and the current Kansas coach, Roy Williams, who played for a season for Smith at Chapel Hill and then coached alongside Smith for 10 years.

Over the years Kansas has produced a prototype kind of team, tough, smart, disciplined. Tradition has turned into trademark. Not surprisingly, the 1996-97 team was one of the school's best, and two of its players, Scot Pollard and Jacque Vaughn, became first-round choices in the NBA draft. If the world of sport has changed dramatically from that time a century ago when a handful of white players gathered around Naismith to experiment with this new and largely unheralded sport, then there is nonetheless a powerful connection to the past that one senses here. College basketball in recent years has gone from something of an athletic afterthought, a wintertime filler between football and baseball seasons, to the nation's new high-profile sport, one which is being embraced at an astonishing rate by the rest of the world. The reason for that growing success is obvious: in an era where the velocity of daily life is ever faster, and where spectators demand more and more action per viewer minute, basketball showcases the fastest, most powerful and most versatile athletes in the world, and it reflects the changes in our society far more accurately than, say, baseball. It is a long way from the simple beginning when Naismith was a young man and Allen was still a boy to today's game with its amazing athletes, its big-time professional salaries, its high-powered college recruiting, its media hype, but it is nice to remember that it all began here. And lest people doubt the influence of Kansas and Allen on the game, they should only remember that it was Phog Allen who probably saved the game for today's stunningly quick and brilliant athletes by preserving its tempo. When other NCAA officials wanted to limit the sport to one dribble per player per possession, something that would have killed the game's speed, it was Allen who mustered the opposition and held the line, opening up the way to the future by that one decision.

Dr. Allen presided on the bench as he did over the eventual careers of players-become-coaches, including Kentucky's famed Adolph Rupp and, later, Ralph Miller, who coached at Wichita State, Iowa and retired at Oregon State.

KU TODAY: THE ROY ERA

BY JOE POSNANSKI

There is something exceedingly wonderful or infuriating about Kansas University basketball, depending on your view. The Jayhawks play selfless basketball, breathtaking basketball, an extra pass here, a jarring pick there, a dive on the floor, all in a fieldhouse so classic the walls sweat. It is too perfect. It is sickeningly perfect. The people cram together and chant their Rock Chalks as the smell of popcorn flutters through the building. Two Jayhawks mascots waddle around, and Kansas scores 10 straight points. From the outside, a stranger must feel like he's pressing his nose against a restaurant window, staring at the stone fireplace and women in silk gowns. He fogs the window glass as he sniffs in vain toward the rack of lamb. People on the outside do hate Kansas basketball.

From the inside, though, it is magic. No, it's more than that. It's love, that's all, unabashed, barefaced, shameless, mushy, corny love, complete with goo-goo eyes and hugs and love letters with circles dotting the I's.

"I wish I could describe what it feels like to be in Allen Fieldhouse when it's packed, when there are so many people it looks like they're going to fall down on top of you," says Jacque Vaughn, a poet, a scholar, Kansas's all-time leader in assists. "I wish I had the words to tell you what that feels like, with the noise all around and my teammates together and Coach Williams on the sidelines, I wish I had the words."

There was this moment toward the end of the 1997 season, just after the glorious regular season, just before the lousy ending. The Jayhawks had won the Big 12 Tournament in Kansas City, only it was more than that. That weekend, they had played a basketball surpassing, as if designed in Roy Williams's dreams. They had suffocated Iowa State, whirled around Missouri, and when the weekend ended they were the best team in America; the best team Williams had ever coached; the best team ever to come out of Kansas. Everything seemed possible.

And they gathered around a stepladder to cut down the championship net, everybody involved, players, coaches, trainers, faculty, congressmen, the cast of *Saturday Night Live,* everybody. And they all snipped away, until finally the net was suspended by one strand. Somebody had to cut it down.

That's when Vaughn pointed at Scot Pollard, who pointed at Jerod Haase, who pointed at Raef LaFrentz, who pointed back at Vaughn. The cheers crashed down. The music thumped through them. Nobody wanted the honor. Pollard pointed at Vaughn, and Vaughn pointed at Billy Thomas, and Thomas pointed at Paul Pierce, and Pierce pointed at Roy Williams, and Williams kept his arms crossed. Haase pointed at his family. C.B. McGrath pointed at the trainer. The trainer pointed at Vaughn. Vaughn pointed at the crowd.

Music rumbled, the pointing continued, the net survived for another minute and another, and now everybody in the building began to laugh. They laughed out loud, deeply, wholeheartedly, the way people laugh at weddings, the way people laugh at the end of *It's a Wonderful Life,* tears trickling down their cheeks. You want to know what it's like on the inside, well, this is it, an arena filled with laughter and tears and music and a championship net dangling by one string.

★ ★ ★

Roy Williams created this hugfest, which is funny because Williams is hardly the Gangster of Love. Williams is a Grandpa Walton type, all shucks and dadgums and advice, straighter than the stretch of Highway 81 between Salina and Wichita. He is exactly the kind of coach who should not connect anymore; the small-town guy who begins each practice with a thought of the day; the old gym rat who stumbles close to tears when watching a player do something particularly unselfish; the sentimental-ist who puts six players on the floor at tipoff of Senior Day because, well, he has six seniors. Coaches like that were supposed to go out in the milkshake days.

Then, there's something else. He's real. Williams has won more games in his first nine years than any coach ever, he has taken two teams to the Final Four, he has been offered millions to coach in the NBA — "Twenty times what I'm making now," he says — and still he is the kid who grew up in the North Carolina mountains, clinging to his mother, Mimmie. He is the kid wandering to Biltmore Elementary to shoot baskets and later keeping statistics for Dean Smith at North Carolina. When Williams coached high school basketball in Asheville, his hometown, he would have barbecues at his house. His wife, Wanda, would make sand-wiches for road games. He had heart-to-heart talks. The team won.

Nothing has changed, really. The stage is big-ger, the money better, the fans louder, but Roy Williams still lives for the same things. "Sure, we want to build families," he says. So he coaxes them, pushes them, punishes them, listens. Jacque Vaughn tells of the days after his junior year when he had to decide whether or not to return for one more season. He was distraught. The NBA offered big money. Lawrence offered an extended childhood. The NBA offered bright lights. Lawrence offered shelter. Vaughn stared at the ceiling during sleepless nights. For the first time in his life, he didn't know what to do.

"I opened up to Coach Williams like I've never opened up to anybody else," Vaughn says. "I told him things I would never tell anyone else. He just listened. He never told me what to do. I mean, this is his job at stake. You know what he was think-ing. But he never said anything. Finally, he told me 'Jacque, I'm going to love you whatever you do.' You can't know what that meant to me."

Everything is geared toward family in Williams's world. Watch Williams when his Jayhawks are in trouble. He simply will not call time-out. He will rage, point, stomp or, worst of all, sit squarely in his chair, his eyes burning. Nobody in America hates losing quite as much as Roy Williams. "He gets that vein in his forehead tensed," Scot Pollard would say, "and you know he's really mad."

Still, Williams will not call time-out, no way, even when his Jayhawks do not move their feet on defense or set up for good shots; even when the opponent scores eight or 10 straight points; even when Dick Vitale screams that somebody better get a T.O., or even when the road cheers tumble around them or Allen Fieldhouse falls mute.

There are basketball reasons, of course. Williams hoards his time-outs. He stuffs them in his mattress, and at the end of games he pulls time-out after time-out, like baby pictures, stretching the game to his heart's delight. He believes time-outs are too precious to squander on a rescue mission. To Williams, wasting a time-out to settle down his team is like squander-ing one of the genie's wishes on a cold beer.

There's another reason, though, a bigger one. Williams wants to see how the family will respond to chaos. They must be together, united, brothers. He stands back to see if his point guard will settle down the team. He wants to see if his big man will step up on defense. He wants to see if his forward will raise the slumped shoulders. He wants to see if they talk to each other, yell at each other, coax each other, love each other.

"We win," says Jerod Haase, the tough player Williams most often compares to himself, "because we are a family."

★ ★ ★

The photographer tried to get them to smile, really smile, but nothing is harder than getting col-lege basketball players to break. This was the 1997 team, Williams's pride, the group he says was more like family than any team he had ever coached. The photographer wanted a smile, something natural. The Jayhawks instead tried to look tough, mean, though it's hard to be Bogart when you are eight big men squished together in a lime green convert-ible Cadillac called Marvin.

Actually, they were not all sitting in Marvin. There's no way to get one shy power forward, two academic All-Americans, one father, two backup

Togetherness is a quality many teams claim, but few matched the 1996-97 Jayhawks.

...THERE IS THE STORY FROM HIS CHILDHOOD THAT HE DOES TELL. HE WOULD PLAY BASKETBALL EVERY DAY WITH FRIENDS, AND ON THE WAY HOME THEY WOULD STOP TO GET BOTTLES OF COCA-COLA AT ED'S SERVICE STATION. WILLIAMS WOULD DRINK WATER, INSTEAD. HE DID NOT HAVE THE 10 CENTS.

point guards, one future NBA star, one conscience-free jump shooter and one 7-footer with painted nails into a Caddie, even if it is a convertible — not without a can opener.

"Marvin," says Scot Pollard, the 7-footer and Marvin's owner, "isn't built for eight."

So, they rolled Marvin into the Allen Fieldhouse parking lot, and Jacque Vaughn stretched out on the hood, and Jerod Haase sat on the side, Pollard leaned back in the driver's seat. Raef LaFrentz, the shy forward from Iowa, sat on the lap of Paul Pierce, the brilliant slasher from Inglewood. Everybody squeezed together, sucking in their stomachs, taking up as little space as they could. Meanwhile, they glared at the camera lens as if this was all a very serious matter, very serious indeed, like world hunger.

"Come on guys," the photographer coaxed, and Vaughn offered up his yearbook smile; LaFrentz gazed at the trees; C.B. McGrath, a backup point guards who yells "Pow" whenever he makes a shot in practice, scrunched his eyebrows and scowled. The others pursed their lips together in that look that college kids think embodies fierceness, though the camera usually picks up something closer to stomach flu. The staring contest between camera and players lingered. Neither side blinked.

Then, some guy, some Kansas student, walked by and noticed the scene.

"Hey," the guy yelled. "Why didn't you wait for me?"

Suddenly, Marvin the Caddie shook. Laughter. Screams. Shrieks. Pollard fell backward, and Billy Thomas, the shooter, broke into a big smile, and B.J. Williams, the father, yelled something back, and Vaughn stretched out on the hood, looked right at the camera and offered up his yearbook smile.

"I'm going to miss these guys," Vaughn would say. "Man, I miss them already."

★ ★ ★

Roy Williams adores small kindness. He doesn't talk much about his childhood. His father, Babe, would drink, and sometimes Mimmie would move Roy and his sister, Frances, into the Shamrock Court Motel until things calmed. Eventually, his parents broke up. "I don't want (my father) portrayed as the villain here," Williams told *Sports Illustrated*, and he said little else because Williams, above all, is a private man.

No, he will not talk much about the rough times, but he will talk all day about small kindness, an encouraging letter, a nice phone call, a firm handshake. His high school coach, Buddy Baldwin, would demand and push and yell, but every so often he offered a smile, an encouraging word — and it melted Williams. At North Carolina, Williams was not good enough to make the varsity team, but Dean Smith — the man Williams would admire most — allowed him to sit in during practices, take notes, learn from the best.

Then, there is the story from his childhood that he does tell. He would play basketball every day with friends, and on the way home they would stop to get bottles of Coca-Cola at Ed's service station. Williams would drink water, instead. He did not have the 10 cents. Mimmie asked him about it one afternoon. She worked in the factory during the day, and she washed clothes for people at night. The next morning, she left a dime on the table.

So, is it any wonder that Williams falls for the kids who set picks, the players who dive for loose balls, the ones who, even on a breakaway, give up the basketball to an open teammate? The crowds roar for the LaFrentz dunk, the Vaughn between-the-legs pass, the Greg Ostertag rejection into the second row, but always Williams is looking at the overlooked, the player who performed the small kindness that makes victories.

"Nobody really knows what I'm looking at," he says. "People watch basketball games differently. A fan watches one thing. A coach sees something else. I see a player fight through a pick on defense. I see a player looking for his teammates. I look for unselfishness."

This is what Williams gets. Unselfishness. His 1991 team was not ranked when the season began, but by the end they beat Indiana, Arkansas and North Carolina in succession. It was a Final Four run so remarkable that it still looks like a misprint. He has won more games than any coach in the 1990s, though he has coached only one player who was named first-team All-America, and he never has coached an NBA lottery pick.

"It's amazing how much can be accomplished," he says at the beginning of his first practice every year, "when no one cares who gets the credit."

★ ★ ★

Coaches build teams in different ways. Some strip away the egos and personalities and build army regiments. Others let their teams run free, unbridled, the dispositions and tempers and laughter swirling, a sort of free-form jazz.

Williams meshes things together, sliding weaknesses and strengths together, colliding doubts and poise, always polishing. His 1997 team was a collection of characters. Billy Thomas grew up on other people's couches in Shreveport, La. Raef LaFrentz grew up in an icebox called Monona, Iowa. Paul Pierce went to a school with no grass. Ryan Robertson made nothing but A's and watched *Days of Our Lives'* in St. Charles, Mo.

B.J. Williams told jokes. Jerod Haase scored 16 points the day after his father died because his father would have wanted it that way. Jacque Vaughn kept his bedroom spotless enough to pass military inspection. Scot Pollard, of course, painted his nails, shaved his head and was completely nuts. Vaughn was the best man at Pollard's wedding.

They were so different, all of them, black and white, rich and poor, Southern and Midwestern and Western, tall and short, talented and scrappy. And there was no reason why they loved each other, except they did. They won 34 games, were No. 1 in America, and they hugged tight after the tournament loss to Arizona. "We will be all right," Jacque

Vaughn said. "Families have to overcome heartache."

There is something exceedingly wonderful and infuriating about Kansas basketball, depending on your view. A few weeks after that wild season ended, the seniors played an exhibition game against some alumni at Allen Fieldhouse. The game itself wasn't much. The seniors took turns hugging Williams, the basketball was raggedy, and the 6,000 or so who still had not put away the loss to Arizona cheered politely.

Only then, the public address announcer told

the fans that Paul Pierce would turn down the NBA millions for another season in Lawrence. The roar shook through Allen Fieldhouse. Then, he told the fans that LaFrentz would turn down even more fame and fortune so he could have one more season playing for Roy Williams. Bedlam. The family was staying together, as if anyone could have doubted. Williams shrugged. "Those are special kids," he said.

The man outside will again press his nose against the window. The music plays on at Kansas.

Marvin (the green Cadillac) was an unlikely mascot and sometimes transportation for the 1997 team.

KU TODAY:
A JAYHAWK CLOSE-UP

PHOTOGRAPHS BY RICH CLARKSON

Kansas basketball in the 1990s came under the indelible mark of Roy Williams, who brings a combination of efficiency, camaraderie and privacy to the Jayhawk locker room. In this family enclave, there is a clear understanding of who is in charge. But there are also elements of democracy, trust and always teamwork. They are the character qualities required by the coach and almost always inherent in his recruits. When Williams stands at the blackboard above the Jayhawk carpet, there are no doubters.

Williams's extended family is the team. There is always a moment of quiet thanks after each game before the team engages in a moment of celebration — a very tame mosh pit. Assistant coach Joe Holladay (above) talks with Jacque Vaughn after the game, as does Williams (below) with Billy Thomas.

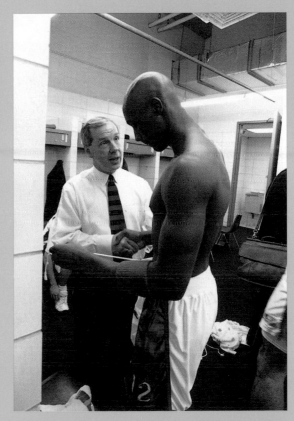

The four years of Jacque Vaughn as point guard were a textbook in guard play and team leadership. But even after four years, sportswriters were still amazed that other textbooks were apparent: How many college basketball players quote Robert Frost at a press conference?

The supporting cast — the red team including B. J. Williams (22) and T. J. Pugh (32) — contribute far more than running the opponent's plays in practice. Playing regularly in big games, they are part of Williams's scheme of substitutions and a deep bench.

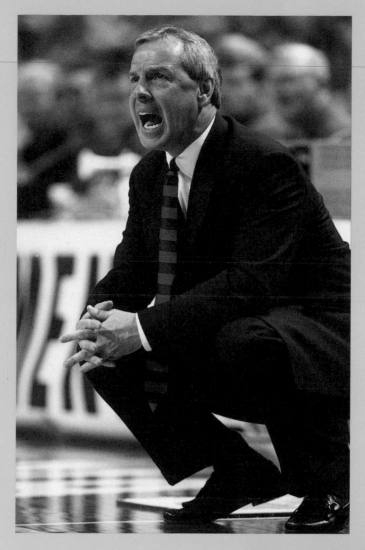

To survive on campus as well as on the court, players must organize themselves in the image of the coach. Before games, the opponent and the game plan are played and replayed in team meetings and in video sessions. When the game begins, Williams pushes the team, but not so far that a free spirit like Scot Pollard (right) cannot joke with his coach.

Williams is often the center of attention. When the team travels, every assistant, student manager and player has an assigned seat on the bus. The coach's "office" is always the front row, right seat. Before and after games, the media surround him for his interpretation of events, past and to come. Even when the team eats together in a favorite restaurant on Lawrence's Iowa Street, kids come up for autographs.

Time-outs are carefully orches-
trated. Players currently in the
game sit down while others stand
behind and are held responsible
for everything discussed. Student

managers have their places and
head manager Jill Johansen puts
the towel on the floor exactly
where Williams will kneel.

Advice comes from everywhere.
This brash student (below)
offers advice to the coach as the
Jayhawks warm up for a league
game in Lincoln, Neb.,
to Williams's good-natured
merriment.

No time is lost. On the bus
back to Lawrence, the team
watches a video replay
(recorded off television) of the
game just concluded.

For all the planning and discipline, when the game heats up, the bench gets involved. This moment, from the end of the 1997 season, was the best and the worst of times: The Jayhawks nearly caught Arizona in the NCAA regional, only to fall just short at the end, in what was considered the upset game of the year. The Wildcats went on to win the national title.

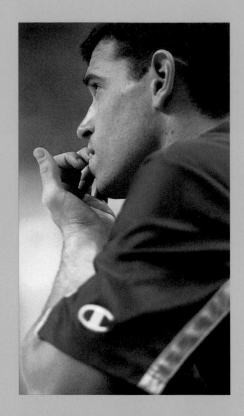

Expressive hands, between drib- tale — particularly when the ban-
bles and jump shots, echo the ten- dage surrounds the fractured wrist
sions of the game. Towels, finger- of Jerod Haase, a key player who
nails and bandages often tell the played with so much pain.

On the road, players dress casually on the bus and in coats and ties the rest of the time. Moments of waiting offer a chance for a quick nap or, more often, for studying. But on many trips, there are historic side excursions to such places as the Eiffel Tower and the battleship *Arizona* at Pearl Harbor. At left, the team begins its tour of the National Civil Rights Museum at Memphis's Lorraine Motel.

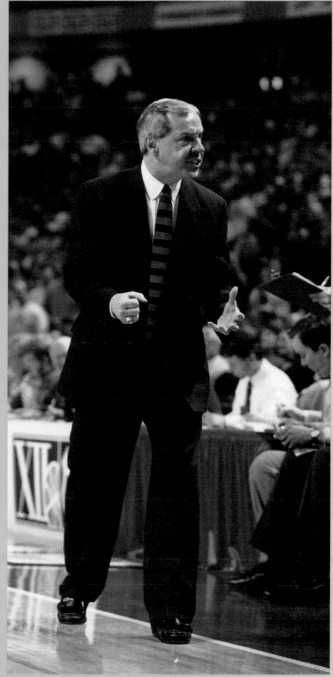

Coach Williams is as intense a game coach as there is in the country. Williams's intensity level can be so high that on several occasions during games when he jumps up and the blood rushes from his head, he nearly blacks out. Williams's players at Kansas have demonstrated the same competitive and focused nature on the court. But at some point — usually when the game is under control — all have fun.

Jayhawks eat well, carefully and often. Pregame meals in Lawrence are served in the Alumni Center (above) with the John Martin mural of previous Kansas All-Americans nearby. Ice cream and cake are served (right) at the Williams's home as the team gathers to watch the

NCAA pairings on television.
On the road, the team often chooses
the restaurant, such as Kansas City's
Majestic Steak House (above right).
But in Birmingham, Williams will
always select his favorite barbecue in
America, Rendezvous Ribs, quite to
the players' approval (bottom right).

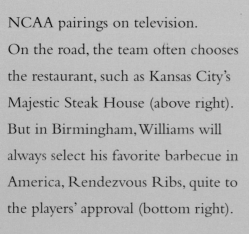

Practices throughout the season include a variety of drills, from weightlifting to rope jumping to stretching — activities designed to keep players in the best condition. On the road, or in Lawrence when Allen Fieldhouse is in other use, team practices are held in the arena of opportunity, which may be Robinson Gym (above right). Wherever, all the equipment travels with the student managers.

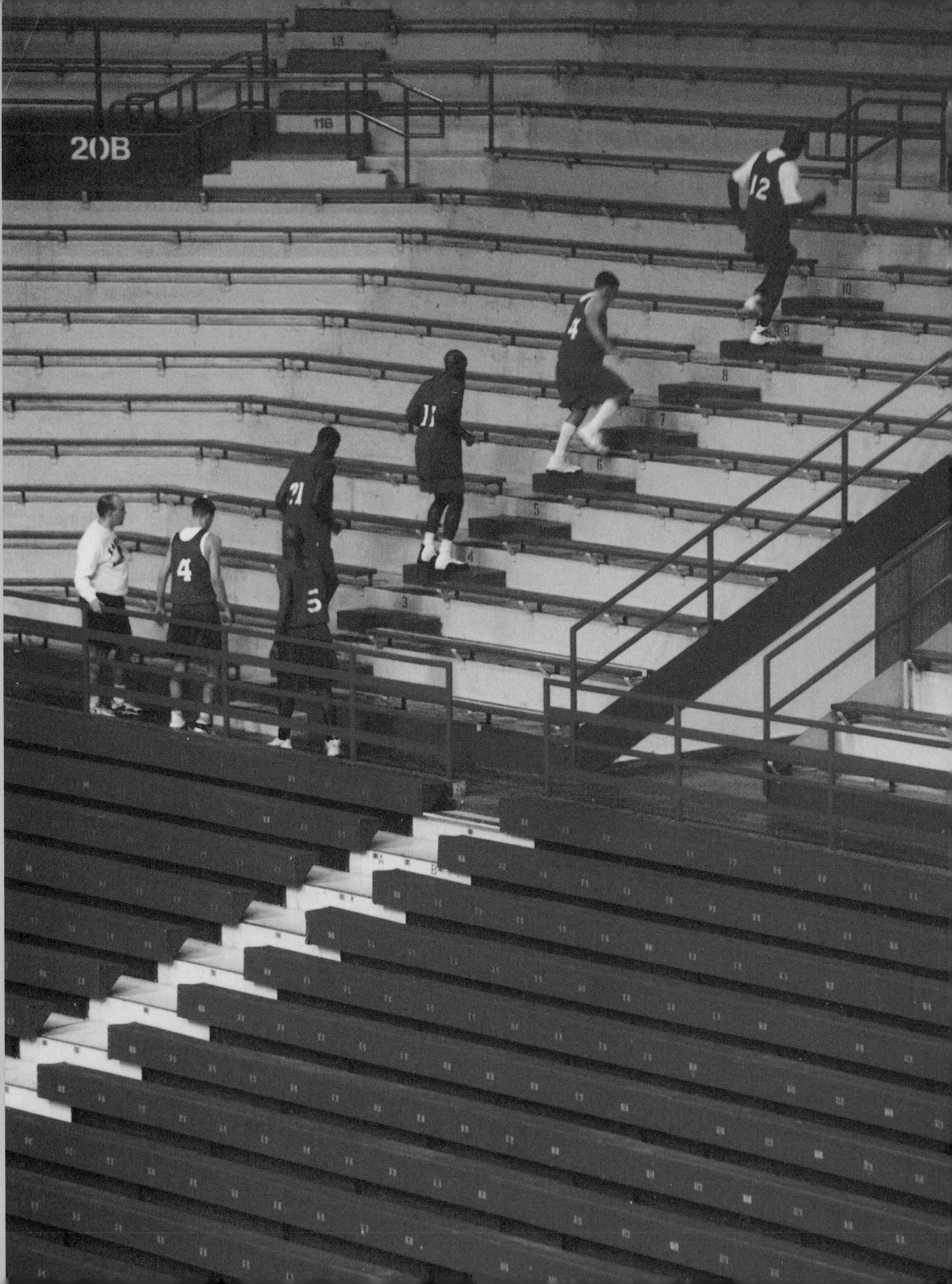
20B
11B

Conditioning continues through-out the season as part of prac-tices. Spectators can watch the practice — quietly and from afar — in Allen Fieldhouse and through the windows of closed doors at Robinson Gym. Practice time is tightly structured with a student manager signaling the end of each period from the day's Practice Plan, which even includes some food for thought.

Before the first-ever Big 12 Conference Tournament title game with Missouri, Raef LaFrentz showed his conference Most Valuable Player hardware, and then after the game, joined his teammates in celebrating their 87-60 victory over the Tigers. The Jayhawks dominated the inaugural event, winning their three tournament games by an average of 22 points.

Memories of KU basketball last forever for the Jayhawk faithful. Among the pieces of history that fans seek are player autographs. Programs, posters, T-shirts and even

skin are places where fans seek their favorite player's signature. The Kansas cheerleaders get the heavily partisan KU crowd at Kansas City's Kemper Arena pumped up before a Big 12 Conference Tournament game. Members of the Jayhawk cheerleading and Crimson Girls dance squads travel to all games, including a trip to Hawaii during the 1996-97 season to root for the Jayhawks during the Maui Classic.

If Allen Fieldhouse has a special reputation, it's because of the fans, particularly the students. Senior Day is a special and emotional event for outgoing Jayhawks. On this final home game of 1997, the six KU seniors — four scholarship and two walk-on players — were honored prior to the Kansas State game. Fans tossed thousands of flowers onto the court in appreciation for what was thought by many to be the finest senior class in Kansas history. But always the

fans get into the game, waving
the wheat and faking indifference
when the opponents are intro–
duced.

Throughout the 1990s, both the writing and broadcast press have surrounded the Jayhawks, as they did at the Big 12 Tournament. There, *The Kansas City Star* had a premade edition announcing the Jayhawks' championship ready for hawkers at the end of the game, and players were reading about their championship (without the details) in the locker room following the game. Moments later, the doors were open to the press for the many interviews. Williams's team stays for interviews until the last sportscaster and writer have every question answered.

When the Jayhawks return on their charter flight to Topeka's Forbes Field, the fans jam the terminal and the players accommodate all before the bus pulls out. Ryan Robertson took nearly 45 minutes to please his fans at the close of the 1997 season. But perhaps one of the most revealing calling cards left by a Williams Kansas team is no calling card at all. When the team has finished the last interview, donned coats and ties for travel, and packed up its gear, the final task is the locker room itself. The used towels are in a pile, the scraps of paper are picked up and the chairs are left in line. And no one but the janitor will know how unique this coach and team really are.

TARHAWKS, JAY HEELS

BY ALEXANDER WOLFF

Kansas and North Carolina would seem to have as much in common as wheat and tobacco; as tornadoes and hurricanes; as flat speech and drawled diction. The states' great universities never even played each other until 1957, when the luck of the draw of the tournament placed both in an epic NCAA final. But each has a basketball history almost as old as the game itself. And if you study basketball's genealogical chart you can trace a direct line from Lawrence to Chapel Hill — from the game's inventor, James Naismith, to its reinventor, Michael Jordan. The Good Doctor begat Jayhawk patriarch Phog Allen, who begat North Carolina coach Dean Smith, who begat His Airness.

Tarhawks, Jay Heels — it's not that there are no differences between the two: It's that one will point so readily and proudly to the other, as if both have been lifelong brothers in some league of the imagination (the Eight-C-C, perhaps?). When the two schools found themselves at the Rainbow Classic in Hawaii in 1992, but not scheduled to play each other, Jayhawks fans cheered for the Tar Heels when North Carolina took on crowd-favorite Michigan, and the Carolina contingent returned the favor when KU faced the host U of H Rainbows, to the further consternation of the locals. Indeed, after Dean Smith was ejected late in the two teams' 1991 national semifinal meeting at the Final Four in Indianapolis, the Tar Heel coach, a graduate of KU's class of 1953, shook hands with the Kansas players and staff before exiting the court. If you're a Jayhawk or a Tar Heel and you must prematurely depart a game involving KU and UNC, you take your leave courteously.

In 1993, as the two schools prepared to play each other in the Final Four for the second time in three seasons, *The Kansas City Star* suggested that "no two Division I programs are more spiritually aligned." Yet consider for a moment only the fleshly connections. In 1983, on the introduction of Smith, Kansas athletic director Monte Johnson hired ex-Tar Heel Larry Brown to coach the Jayhawks. Five years later Brown's successor would be Roy Williams, who grew up in Asheville, N.C., and apprenticed for 10 seasons in Chapel Hill as Smith's assistant. Williams came to the attention of the Kansas A.D., now Bob Frederick, through the UNC coach. (Perhaps Smith should take a tax deduction for alumni giving: Over the 14 seasons in which his spawn have headed up basketball operations in Lawrence, they have coached Kansas to more victories and as many Final Four appearances as their teacher himself has delivered for Carolina.)

But there are powerful emotional ties, too. When Williams was a pup of an assistant at Chapel Hill, he earned extra bucks delivering videotapes of Smith's weekly TV show by navigating the state in an old jalopy. Hearing of the Tar Heel assistant's moonlighting, Michael Jordan's father, James, voiced his concern. "Hope you pull over if you feel sleepy," Papa Jordan told Williams. "When I go for long drives, that's what I do."

Years later, now at Kansas, Williams would get word that James Jordan, after pulling over for just such a nap on a Carolina country road, had been murdered. Nothing could have more quickly transported Williams from his adopted state back to his native one.

Many other ties bind the two schools and states. Current KU assistant Matt Doherty wears a championship ring picked up at Chapel Hill. William's son Scott and Frederick's son Brad were briefly teammates on the Carolina basketball jayvee. Smith's classmate and friend at Topeka High was KU alum-to-be and future U.S. senator Nancy Landon Kassebaum.

But no moment sits more squarely at the center of this pale-blue/royal-blue relationship than the 1957 NCAA final, in which the top-ranked and unbeaten Tar Heels defeated the No. 2, Wilt Chamberlain-led Jayhawks 54-53 in triple overtime. And that brings up another figure with one foot in Lawrence and another in Chapel Hill.

By the 1950s Dick Harp had become the top assistant to Allen, assuming a more and more important behind-the-scenes role in running the Jayhawk program. Allen still worked hard to lure young men to Lawrence, and he still motivated them on game days. But Harp was the *eminence grise* of Kansas's 1952 NCAA title, the man credited with developing the half-court press that helped the Jayhawks ease past Frank McGuire's St. John's team, 80-63, in the final.

[We interrupt this narrative to bring you a Kansas-Carolina bonus trivia question. Who are the only two coaches to have taken two different schools to an NCAA championship game? The answer: Brown (UCLA in 1980 and Kansas in '88) and McGuire (the Johnnies in '52 and the Tar Heels in '57 — both, curiously enough, against Kansas). Soon after McGuire moved to Chapel Hill, Brown would play for him and Smith would serve as his assistant.]

By the 1956-57 season, Harp's first in charge in Lawrence, Smith was now an assistant at the Air Force Academy. That March he roomed with his boss, Falcons coach Bob Spear, and McGuire in Kansas City at the Final Four. Two years later Smith would join McGuire in Chapel Hill, but here, during the championship game, he cheered unabashedly for his alma mater. After all, four years earlier Smith had coached three of the Jayhawks' current seniors, Gene Elstun, Maurice King and John Parker, on the KU freshman team.

Thus Smith was as disappointed with the UNC victory as Harp, whose team finished a 24-3 season only five points and eight seconds short of perfection. For years afterward Harp would blame himself

for his team's failure to get the ball into Chamberlain during the final, and he would persist in describing the game as one the Jayhawks "coulda won, shoulda won."

Like Smith, who had grown up in Emporia and Topeka, Harp spent his childhood in the Kansas City, Kansas, neighborhood of Rosedale, listening to Jayhawk games on the radio before coming to Lawrence and making his mark as a basketball player. In 1986, now long since ensconced at North Carolina as head coach, Smith brought Harp to Chapel Hill as an administrative assistant coach. Over the three seasons Harp spent with the Tar Heels' program, Carolinians would occasionally bring up the events of '57, and that wasn't much fun. But Harp was integral to North Carolina's two ACC regular-season titles and one ACC tournament championship over that span, and a circle, in a sense, had been closed.

Since Smith arrived in Chapel Hill, the two schools haven't gone out of their way to play one another. They have faced each other only seven times in the 40 years since their first, unforgettable meeting. (The Tar Heels lead the series 5-2.) But only two of those games have occurred since Smith's proteges took up in Lawrence; both were unavoidable encounters in postseason play, in the national semifinals of the NCAA tournament. "Why play against someone you consider a friend?" Smith says. A situation in which the joy of victory gets complicated by sorrow for the vanquished coach is something, Williams adds, that "we don't need to schedule." The stat sheet from their messy meeting at the '91 Final Four — sub-40% shooting; 30-plus turnovers — makes clear that neither was really up for doing battle against the other.

The two programs are family in their own fashion, so better that they march onward and upward in parallel, like spouses, for better or for worse. When Dean Smith's old classmate Nancy Landon Kassebaum remarried in 1997, there was only one thing wrong with the occasion. Her groom, Howard Baker, was a former U.S. senator from . . . Tennessee.

When Dean Smith cuts the Final Four nets, it's the next best thing to a Jayhawk trophy.

In the late '70s, Dean Smith had assistant Bill Guthridge on one elbow and Eddie Fogler on the other. And close at hand was Roy Williams, who during his 10-year stint at Carolina saw the Tar Heels make 10 NCAA appearances and win six ACC championships.

Twice in the '90s including here in 1993, Williams and Smith shook hands before a NCAA national semifinal game matching Carolina and Kansas. In the 1993 game, Greg Ostertag and Adonis Jordan (30) blocked Derick Phelps's path to the basket, but it wasn't enough to keep the Tar Heels from winning 78-68 on their way to the national championship. Though, in a way, everything was in the family.

In 1991, the Jayhawks defeated the Tar Heels 79-73 behind the play of Adonis Jordan (30) and Mark Randall (42), who celebrated the national semi-final victory. Unranked in preseason polls, Kansas defeated No. 3-ranked Indiana and No. 2-ranked Arkansas to get to the Carolina game. The victory before 47,100 fans in Indianapolis's Hoosierdome set up the championship matchup with the Duke Blue Devils. KU's bubble burst as Duke won the championship 72-65.

Gene Budig celebrates a KU national championship.

GOVERNORS AND CHANCELLORS

It was good politics to sit center court at KU basketball games to see and be seen. Senators, legislators and mayors could be seen in their prime seats. But governors in particular seemed to rake in the most political hay. Alf Landon loved Jayhawk games and attended them regularly as long as his health permitted. Later governors also followed Kansas basketball, often going to the locker room after the games to congratulate the team in person.

KU chancellors all have a special place in their hearts for Jayhawk basketball. A winning basketball team raises the morale of not just the student body and faculty but also of the alumni, some of whom respond with either advice or checkbooks, as the moment suggests.

Gov. Bob Docking presents a Big 8 trophy.

Gov. Bill Avery congratulates players in the postgame locker room.

Chancellor Laurence Chalmers enjoys a moment of victory with coach Ted Owens.

Chancellor W. Clarke Wescoe watches
the Jayhawks with cigar and son.

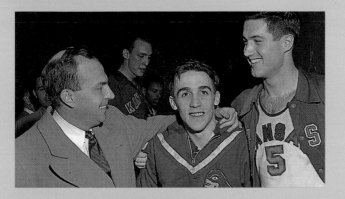

Dr. Franklin D. Murphy embraces champions
Dean Kelley and Charlie Hoag.

Current Chancellor Robert Hemenway consults with
Athletic Director Bob Frederick and Coach Williams.

Gov. Bill Graves calls on the Jayhawks in the
locker room after a Big 12 conference game in 1997.

MORE THAN PEACH BASKETS

BY JOHN MCLENDON

My father told me about Kansas University and some of the problems I might run into as a black student in 1933. When he took me to the school, he told me to go find Dr. Naismith. "Tell him that he's to be your adviser," my father said.

I did just that, and Dr. Naismith said, "Who told you this?"

"My father," I said.

"Fathers are always right," Dr. Naismith said.

Many of my doubts about being at Kansas were quickly dispelled by Dr. Naismith, who treated me courteously and attentively and made me feel comfortable in my surroundings as a new student.

Dr. Naismith was in his 70s at the time, having been allowed to remain as a member of the KU faculty by a state legislative act. He was given the right to teach for as long as he wanted at Kansas. His class in health instruction was required, but very popular. It was an open forum that he conducted rather informally, discussing any and all topics. He once was called before the dean to explain why he had given so many A's in his class. "Anybody that came to my class deserved a good grade if they had to listen to me," he told the dean.

This certainly was a modest statement, because Dr. Naismith had already acquired Ed.D., Ph.D. and doctor of divinity degrees. In addition to serving as my adviser, Dr. Naismith was my teacher in physical education, anatomy and kinesiology, which dealt with the analysis of motion and its application and was his favorite subject.

But Dr. Naismith taught me far more than was found in textbooks. Very often he would put aside his books and teach us lessons in life from his world experiences. And that always included how he happened to invent the game of basketball in 1891.

After he had earned his doctor of divinity degree from McGill College in Montreal, Dr. Naismith went to the Springfield YMCA College in Massachusetts as a physical trainer. One of his instructors there told him he could use the YMCA experience to better the lives of young people just as well as he could lecturing from the pulpit.

At the time, the Y was searching for a game to

John McLendon, a native of Hiawatha, Kans., became the first black to graduate with a degree in physical education from KU in 1936. A keen student of the game, he became one of basketball's most respected coaches. From 1957 to 1959, his Tennessee State teams became the first to win three consecutive NAIA titles. He also coached at North Carolina Central, Hampton Institute, Kentucky State and Cleveland State, amassing a 523-165 record over 25 years. He was the first coach from historically black colleges to enter the Naismith Memorial Hall of Fame. The honor was especially appropriate for McLendon, who was deeply affected by Naismith's philosophy, techniques and thorough distaste for segregation.

fill the off-season time for football players who had too much energy and were disrupting the dorms at night.

Dr. Naismith conceived a game, with 18 players divided into two teams — three guards, three center, three wings — and two 15-minute halves. They would pass the ball around — dribbling was a foul and so was taking more than one step with the ball — and try to throw the ball into elevated targets at either end of the court. If you committed two fouls, you had to sit out until someone on either side made a shot.

The custodian of the YMCA, a man named Stebbins, brought a ladder to the first game, propped it against a wall and stood on the ladder "tending to the goal" — the first goaltender, so to speak — to retrieve the ball after a successful shot. He also talked Dr. Naismith into letting him substitute peach baskets for boxes. Dr. Naismith was the referee, timekeeper and scorekeeper, but the records show there was only one basket made in the first game — on the last shot of the game!

Believing that players should make up their own strategy, Dr. Naismith did not feel that coaches were necessary to play his game. Players would decide how to attack the basket. Dr. Naismith also believed it wasn't fair or Christian to take advantage of opponents and had rules against pushing, shoving and holding — rules that are still in effect today. He really believed sports taught a person how to be more honest and fair and that competition brought out your character. He also found that the game could teach other tools for life.

But it wasn't until Dr. Naismith came to Kansas that a creative student named Forrest Allen showed him the value of a coach in directing players. Dr. Naismith gave Phog Allen the title of "father of basketball coaching."

Dr. Naismith was an inventive teacher. He would take his class out on the highway. There he would conduct an experiment to show us how to measure the kinesthetic sense of an individual and how it could be a predictor of physical skill. The method he used was to have us drive a car at about 35 miles an hour and then try to eliminate various factors like vibration, sight, feeling and hearing while we were driving the car to test our kinesthetic sense. If you could sustain the speed of a car at 35 miles an hour while blindfolded, with your ears clogged or sitting inside an inner tube, according to Dr. Naismith, you had great kinesthetic sense as an athlete. His experiment was interrupted

because of the 1936 Berlin Olympics, which he attended to celebrate basketball's official inclusion as part of the medal program.

Dr. Naismith wanted his men not only to be he-men, as he would call them, but gentlemen. He deplored any form of discrimination, segregation or prejudice, and helped me to surmount glaring institutional discriminatory practices during my junior and senior years.

The first involved my attempt to enroll in a required subject, practice teaching. As the first black physical education student enrolled in the school, it would be difficult for me to teach students at segregated schools, so I asked to be excused from practice teaching.

When I told Dr. Naismith about my problem, he told me to come back in a day or two and we might have an answer. I returned and he presented a plan for me.

I would begin my practice teaching at once, he said, even though I was a junior and this was usually just for seniors. He said it would be better for me to do practice teaching for two years since they might give me only one-half credit for the plan he had in mind. The attitude prevailing in the state was that white students were not to be taught by black teachers, but he proposed for me to get my experience on three different levels — elementary school, junior high school and senior high school — in both segregated and integrated physical education classes.

So I was assigned by Dr. Naismith to do my practice teaching at Lincoln Elementary School, a segregated school in North Lawrence. At the same time, on other days of the week, he sent me to Lawrence Junior High, an integrated school, where I was to teach gymnastics. After Thanksgiving, I would go to basketball practice at Liberty Memorial Senior High School, an integrated school with separate white and black teams, as an assistant basketball coach.

Dr. Naismith's plan was for me to get my experience, in effect, by circumventing the existing system but gaining the valuable teaching experience on a number of different levels. Although I never saw the white team, by my senior year I was made the head coach of the black team at Lawrence Memorial and we won the Kansas-Missouri Athletic Conference championship. It was after watching my coaching efforts that Dr. Naismith said, "Whatever you do in physical education, stick with this game."

There's no question that my life would not

As with modern-day coaches, Dr. Naismith appreciated the height advantage. He is shown here with player William Johnson.

have been anywhere near what it has become if I had not met Dr. Naismith. He never looked at life as black and white. One thing he taught in the adjustment to adversity is that no matter what kind of problem you had, never let it defeat you. Even though you may not think something is fair or just, you can't let that stop you. You just try to get around it.

Dr. Naismith's attitude may not be viewed as modern by today's standards; people have learned the method of protest to bring pressure on those who make the rules. Others may just let a problem keep them from their goals and positive direction. His philosophy was that adversity is just another opportunity. That may sound naive, but it worked for me then and it still applies today.

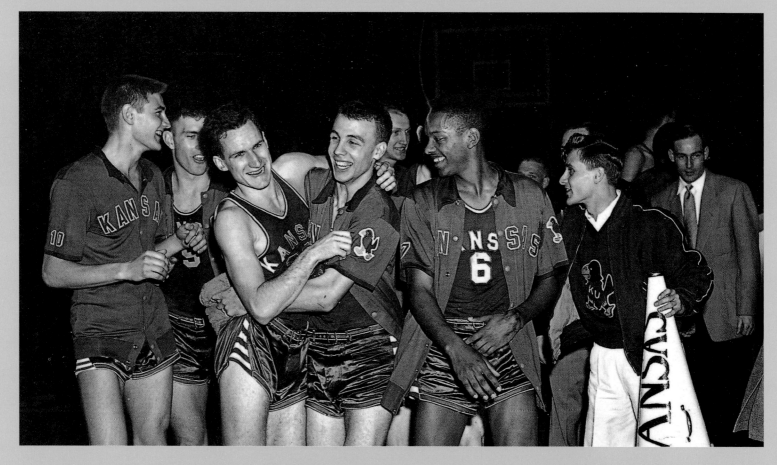

LaVannes Squires was part of a celebrating team that included (from the left) Jerry Alberts, Dean Smith and Al Kelley.

*A*lthough he was a good enough athlete, McLendon was not allowed to play basketball for KU in 1936 because he was black. It seems inconceivable today that blacks were not welcomed then by many teams, both college and professional.

And it took 16 more years until Kansas welcomed its first black player. LaVannes Squires, a 6-foot forward who had played high school ball for coach Ralph Miller at Wichita East, suited up for KU home games during the 1951-52 championship season. Squires, nicknamed "Scooter" by his teammates, was accepted without any undue attention. The historic milestone went almost unnoticed until the following year when Squires made the traveling squad for a double-header with Southern Methodist in Dallas. The team stayed in an elegant hotel near the campus.

One of the assistant managers of the hotel pulled Dr. Allen aside as the team was preparing for its pregame meal and suggested that Squires eat in the kitchen.

"Then, set places for all of us in the kitchen," Dr. Allen said and he walked off.

The entire team ate in the dining room.

The Rules

1. The ball may be thrown in any direction with one or both hands.

2. The ball may be batted in any direction with one of both hands (never the fist).

3. A player cannot run with the ball. The player must throw it from the spot on which he catches it; allowance to be made for a man who catches the ball when running at a good speed.

4. The ball must be held in or between the hands; the arms or body must not be used for holding it.

5. No shouldering, holding, pushing, tripping, or striking, in any way the person of an opponent shall be allowed; the first infringement of this rule by any person shall count as a foul, the second shall disqualify him until the next goal is made, or if there was evident intent to injure the person for the whole of the game, no substitute allowed.

6. A foul is striking at the ball with the fist, violation of Rules 3, 4, and such as described in Rule 5.

7. If either side makes three consecutive fouls, it shall count as a goal for the opponents.

8. A goal shall be made when the ball is thrown or batted from the grounds into the basket and stays there, providing those defending the goal do not touch or disturb the goal. If the ball rests on the edge and the opponent moves the basket, it shall count as a goal.

9. When the ball goes out of bounds, it shall be thrown into the field and played by the first person touching it. In case of a dispute, the umpire shall throw it straight into the field. The thrower-in is allowed five seconds. If he holds it longer it goes to the opponent. If any side persists in delaying the game, the umpire shall call a foul on them.

10. The umpire shall be judge of the players and shall note the fouls and notify the referee when three consecutive fouls have been made. He shall have the power to disqualify players according to Rule 5.

11. The referee shall be the judge of the ball and shall decide when the ball is in play, in bounds, to which side it belongs, and shall keep the time. He shall decide when a goal has been made, and keep account of the goals, with any other duties that are usually performed by a referee.

12. The time shall be two fifteen-minute halves, with five minutes rest between them.

13. The side making the most goals in that time shall be declared the winners. In case of a draw, the game may, by agreement of the captains, be continued until another goal is made.

Naismith posed for pictures many times with the peach basket, along with Dr. Allen and KU players. Little did Naismith realize that those original rules of the game he wrote back in Springfield, Mass., would bring him the modest fame he experienced at Kansas, much less the growth of his game.

THE ARENAS

Basketball was played on the Kansas campus from 1898 until 1907 in the basement of "old Snow Hall," which was located just north of where Watson Library is today. The west portion of the basement was where Naismith introduced the game to Kansans in "the large room." But unfortunately, the large room had low ceilings, so the first games were played in downtown Lawrence at either the armory, the skating rink or the YMCA — whichever was available at the time.

Robinson Gymnasium was the first real home of the Jayhawks, and for 25 years the team played in Robinson's second floor that also housed the athletic offices. For games, bleachers were brought in for the sidelines, and fans craned to watch the action from the running track in the balcony. As many as 900 fans would cram themselves into Robinson's tight quarters. Even after the games moved to Hoch Auditorium, Robinson still served as the practice floor. Here, a practice takes place in 1908.

The first real basketball home for the Jayhawks was the second floor of Robinson Gymnasium. For 25 years the Jayhawks played in Robinson's tight quarters, until the completion of Hoch Auditorium in the mid-'30s. Even then, many practice sessions were held in Robinson, and the team locker rooms were located there until 1955 when Allen Fieldhouse was completed. Hoch was truly a multipurpose building, hosting basketball, concerts and convocations. The sloping floor leading to the stage stopped where the flat basketball court was installed. Bleachers were moved onto the stage for games. With standing room, all of 3,800 people could watch a game.

But Hoch was still an auditorium. The two team benches were separated by not just the scorer's table but also the console of Hoch's huge pipe organ. The stage curtains were pulled high, and lights for the basketball floor were low-

ered on cords from the arched ceiling. The full 125-piece band sat in the center of the stage. For fans sitting on the opposite side, Hoch's sloping floor and two high balconies provided great acoustics when Director Russell Wiley conducted "For I'm a Jay, Jay, Jay, Jayhawk."

Securing funds for the construction of Allen Fieldhouse was a task beset by many difficulties. Critics scoffed at its size, not to mention its cost. Even the need for insuring the building became controversial. But the biggest stumbling block at the time was the difficulty of getting the steel girders during materiel shortages of the Korean War.

The dedication of Allen Fieldhouse on March 1, 1955, was a unique celebration in KU history. Many players from earlier teams returned to join the 17,228 fans who attended. Gov. Ed Arn, Chancellor Franklin D. Murphy and the man for whom the building was named, Forrest C. "Phog" Allen, all

Hoch Auditorium was designed as a music hall and the flat basketball floor was an afterthought. Hoch's soaring stage accommodated symphony orchestras, operas and large traveling road shows. Because Hoch was normally used as an auditorium, the most famous of all Kansas players to play on its floor, Clyde Lovellette, was nicknamed the "Monster of the Music Hall." In 1938 (left), netting was erected to protect the glass chandeliers behind the baskets. And in 1952, fans watched from the stage bleachers as legendary Oklahoma A&M coach Henry Iba attempted to influence a foul call on Kansas's Harold Patterson.

spoke before the game and at halftime.

The capacity of the fieldhouse at its dedication was 17,300, which made it the largest campus arena in the country for many years. (Capacity was later modified and Allen Fieldhouse today seats 1,000 less.)

The dedication game was memorable for all who were there, which included the entire Kansas legislature. The ceremonies lengthened the halftime, and the two teams rehashed their second half strategies over and over. But the second half was just right for the Jayhawks, as they defeated rival Kansas State 77-67.

On that night and after each game until Dr. Allen retired, dignataries and fans would surround him for up to an hour. On one of those occasions, only a few days after the inaugural game, Joe Skillman, chief of the campus police, approached the coach with bad news. Fire from a dropped cigarette had started in the front seat of his brand new Cadillac, a gift at the dedication dinner. The interior was now in ashes.

Luckily, it was insured.

Opponents have always complained that tournament games in Kansas City were home games for Kansas. Indeed, the short trip up the highway insured good crowds when the Jayhawks played there. Kansas City's old Municipal Auditorium was the site of many preseason tournaments, NCAA regionals and finals. When the Jayhawks and their fans arrived, the lobby of the Muehlebach Hotel became the Kansas headquarters before and after games. Big 6 Commissioner Reeves Peters's office was on the hotel mezzanine, and the teams all stayed at the Muehlebach, the Continental and the Phillips. The preseason tournament held between Christmas and New Year's also drew good crowds from Missouri and Kansas State, which set the stage for intense rivalries. One year when Mizzou, K-State and the Jayhawks were all defeated in first-round play, a headline writer at *The Kansas City Star* struggled to get the defeats into a one-column headline. His solution: "Plenty of Tickets."

BEWARE OF THE PHOG

BY TED O'LEARY

My last year at Kansas was 1932. We started 2-3 in the Big Six and were about out of it. I thought the team was too stressed out, too tense. We used to put our hands together, give a big cheer, that sort of stuff. Our coach, Doc Allen, believed in that, he thought it was great. I went to him and said that I thought we were too tight when we went on the court and that cheering stuff was part of the reason. I thought we'd be better off just sort of lounging around before the games and at least acting like we were more relaxed. He went along with it. That showed me he was willing to be flexible and he'd listen to his players. I don't know how he was later in his career, but I'll never forget the way he treated us. He thought a lot of his players and cared for them when they were on the team and after they left school.

It seems incredible now that I got to know two of the most important people in basketball, Doc and James Naismith. Whenever I mention to anybody that I knew Naismith they become transfixed. It seems nobody thought of him as a person who actually lived, or who lived in Kansas. I can see why. He invented the game in Massachusetts and that's where the Naismith Hall of Fame is. He didn't do anything famous in Kansas, but after basketball became popular everybody was kind of proud that the guy who invented the game was on our campus. When I worked at *Sports Illustrated*, they were all fascinated about my knowing Naismith.

I'm a faculty brat. My father taught literature and writing at Kansas for 40 years. We knew all the other professors, and we knew Naismith like we knew any other teacher. I had Naismith for a sexual hygiene class, a compulsory class. Dull, boring. Naismith was bored teaching it. He called roll for a class of 400 and 398 would answer present and 200 of them would be answering for the others. We got a true-false test at the end.

Theodore "Ted" O'Leary is one of the last links to James Naismith. O'Leary grew up in Lawrence, where he was a high school track star, and attended Kansas from 1928 to 1932. O'Leary, like all incoming KU freshmen, took a physical education class with Naismith as the instructor. O'Leary was a standout basketball player and co-captain of the 1932 Big Six championship team. He was selected to one of the first All-America teams, chosen by College Humor *magazine. After graduating, O'Leary coached at George Washington for two seasons and compiled a 26-9 record.*

But writing was in his blood. He returned to Kansas City and worked as a reporter for The Kansas City Star *until entering the Navy in 1942. After the war, he returned to journalism in many capacities. He edited a hobbies magazine, wrote segments for encyclopedias, was a longtime Kansas City correspondent for* Sports Illustrated *and reviewed books for the* Star *for nearly a half-century. Some 18,000 books are stacked to the ceilings in several rooms of his Fairway, Kans., home. One of O'Leary's final freelance stories was a 1973 feature on his old coach, Phog Allen, for the* Star. *O'Leary remembered Phog as being mostly alert for man of 87 and typically irascible, just as he had been in his coaching days. Allen died a year later. Memories of Naismith, Allen and Kansas basketball are kept alive through O'Leary, who has digested about 15,000 of the books in his house.*

DOC WAS ONE OF A KIND. HE MADE BASKETBALL A JOY TO PLAY. I NEVER STEPPED ON THE BASKETBALL COURT WITH ANYTHING BUT ANTICIPATION OF A GREAT EXPERIENCE.

Naismith was a quiet man who knew plenty about every sport, not just basketball. I don't think Naismith really gave a damn about basketball as a spectator game. He came to all the games, sat on the second row at Hoch Auditorium and hardly ever changed his expression. He never applauded, just sat there and watched the game he created. It was far more interesting to him to teach fencing to a small group. And he was fascinated by wrestling.

Of course, Phog Allen was just the opposite. Basketball meant everything to him. Our family was close to the Allens. They moved to Lawrence from Warrensburg, Mo., in 1919 when Doc (former players refer to Allen as Doc) got the job as athletic director. My mother was always good about befriending the families of the new faculty members. Doc appreciated that. We were neighbors, and my best friend for a while was Forrest Allen Jr. He died of typhoid fever when we were in junior high. I was a pallbearer at his funeral. The incident brought our families even closer together.

Doc was one of a kind. He made basketball a joy to play. I never stepped on the basketball court with anything but anticipation of a great experience.

My attitude about his coaching has changed over the years. It actually was very simple. He talked about his stratified man-to-man defense with zone principles, which sounded fancy but was simple, really. Our first two or three weeks of practice we would do nothing but fundamentals. We'd pivot, throw hook passes, bounce passes. We did that for two or three hours a day. Practice was so monotonous. But it paid off. We handled the ball better than the teams we played.

Once the season started we did two things every practice. We shot baskets for one and a half hours and scrimmaged for one and a half hours. We never had any great plays. Doc was a free-lance

coach who taught free-lance offense. He relied on getting great players and teaching and drilling. We'd drill on fundamentals of shooting and passing. Then every practice would end with everybody shooting 100 free throws.

One thing he told me typified his attention to detail. He always wore a warm-up suit on the court. When I played, most coaches didn't do that. I once asked him why and he said he liked to demonstrate shots, and that if he were to come out in street clothes and make a shot we'd think it was lucky. But, when he dressed like one of the players we'd

Ray Evans (left) and Otto Schnellbacher were two football greats Dr. Allen enticed to join the basketball squad when the football season ended.

THE PLAYERS ALL RESPECTED DOC. HE WAS A GOOD HANDBALL PLAYER. IF HE FOUND OUT YOU'D BEEN OUT ON A WEEKEND AND HAD A FEW BEERS HE'D CALL AND TELL YOU HE'D WANT TO MEET YOU ON THE HANDBALL COURT AT 1 P.M. THE NEXT DAY. HE'D GET YOU OUT THERE, RUN YOU RAGGED . . .

pay attention to what he was saying. And he could shoot. He had this underhand shot. He was amazing with it. We all shot our free throws underhanded. For long shots we used two-handed set shots.

We did do some different things occasionally. One year he put in two special out-of-bounds plays from under the basket. We practiced and practiced those and they worked maybe three times all season. About 20 years later I was at a practice when Doc was getting ready for an NCAA Tournament game. He called me over and said, "This is Ted O'Leary. He scored 24 baskets himself on this out of bounds play for us one year." They believed him.

Sometimes he got a little absentminded. Once, he diagrammed a play with a X's and O's and he put six O's up on the board. I raised my hand and asked him who was going to cover that sixth O. He didn't like that very much.

I can't imagine a better motivator. Before a game and at halftime, motivation probably was his strongest suit. I was told the old New York manager John McGraw said the same thing about wearing a Giants uniform, but Doc would convince you that when you put on a Jayhawks uniform you were meant to win, that it would be a fluke if you didn't win.

There was a night playing Colorado when we were down eight or nine at halftime. We knew we were going to get a tongue lashing because we hadn't played very well. We sat in the locker room waiting and waiting for him, but he never showed. Then with two minutes left in the intermission I told the team that Doc doesn't have to tell us what to do, that we knew what we were doing wrong and we'd have to fix it on our own. We couldn't always rely on him. He told me later that's what he intended, and he used that ploy throughout his career.

There was a game he turned into a story. The motivational aspect was typically Doc, and so was the fabrication of the story. We had to beat Oklahoma at Hoch in the final game and Kansas State had to beat Missouri for us to win the 1932 Big Six championship outright. We weren't going to have our best player, Bill Johnson. He was attending his father's funeral in Oklahoma City in the afternoon and the game was at night. We assumed that after such a somber occasion Bill probably wouldn't want to play, but Doc would have none of that.

Doc pushed back our game time by an hour and told people he wanted to give our fans a chance to listen to the important Kansas State-Missouri game. What really happened was he had arranged with an Oklahoma City booster to fly Johnson to Lawrence after the funeral and wanted to give him the extra hour. Before the game, he told us Johnson was coming but we weren't to tell anybody. We didn't want Oklahoma to find out. Bill got there in time for final warmups, but Doc told him to go over to Robinson Gym and warm up by himself. About 10 minutes before game time, who would walk down the Hoch Auditorium steps but Bill Johnson. The crowd went mad. The faces on the OU guys fell. I'd never seen a team deflated like that. The great anticlimax is Bill fouled out and never really was much of a factor in the game. We won the game, but Doc never stressed that part when he retold the story.

Doc told many stories. Throughout his life, he was always interesting to talk to. He loved to tell the story about the (1904) games between the Buffalo Germans and the Kansas City Athletic Club, a series he arranged and starred in. The Athletic Club won, and basketball really took off in Kansas City. Those were the earliest days of organized basketball. Doc would tell stories about how the Germans had an iron cage around their court and their trick was to push opponents into the cage. That's how they won so many games. Doc loved those kind of stories.

You'd strike up a conversation with him about an opposing player or team and he'd go off talking about why Prohibition should be repealed, why the price of eggs is so high this year, and why the French produce the best wine. Then he'd come back to the player and team. He had a remarkable gift of gab and was a picturesque talker. He called the AAU folks, who pretty much ran the U.S. Olympic team, "trans-Atlantic hitchhikers." Tall players were "mezzanine Peeping Toms." Doc thought tall players would ruin basketball. Of course that didn't preclude him from recruiting Clyde Lovellette and Wilt Chamberlain, who were the best big men of their day. And even when I played he got a player named Harry Kersenbrock, who was a 7-footer from Nebraska, to transfer from a small college. Kersenbrock would have been basketball's first giant. He was on campus, and I was just fascinated by him. But the summer before he was supposed to play for us, he drowned in a creek, and it broke up Doc very much. We had our worst season that year.

The players all respected Doc. He was a good handball player. If he found out you'd been out on a weekend and had a few beers he'd call and tell you he'd want to meet you on the handball court at 1 p.m. the next day. He'd get you out there, run you ragged, then he'd push you into a corner and tell you he'd heard you'd been out and let this be a lesson to you. That happened to me. Then I got pretty good at handball and I beat him. He wanted a rematch and I beat him again. He never called to play me again.

Doc stayed on his players about smoking and drinking. He said he did that as a teenager and it almost ruined him and he saw the light. He ingrained it into everybody that smoking and drinking were venal sins because they hurt your conditioning so badly. He'd suspend a guy for smoking. In the 1950s, the first year after Doc retired, I saw Doc in the lobby of Municipal Auditorium between halves of a game smoking a cigarette. I couldn't believe it. He had done an incredible job hiding it from us all those years.

This wouldn't happen today. We played Kansas State, and it was the first time I started a game. They had a good player named Elden Auker, who went

on to pitch in the major leagues. Auker and I went for a ball and my finger split open. I got taped up and went back in the game. We won the game and I was high scorer so I didn't think much about my finger until I got home that night and then I felt the pain. About 10:30 there's a knock on my door and it's Doc. He had me soak my hand in Epsom salts and stayed with me until it felt better. I can't imagine a coach today taking care of his players like that.

All his players called him Doc. He was Phog to the reporters and then everybody started calling him that. But he was Doc to us. He fixed us all up and he gave us rubdowns. Our practices would end around six, and he'd give every starting player a 15-minute rubdown. He was our trainer as well as our coach, and he was trainer for a lot of other athletes. People like Mickey Mantle and Johnny Mize went to see him, but during my time he'd see players like Grover Cleveland Alexander. He had quite a reputation among the baseball players. Doc was especially good with back injuries.

More than anything, I remember Doc being somebody who was ahead of his time in so many ways. He made basketball exciting at Kansas; he treated injuries because he believed healthy teams would be in better shape to win; he thought basketball could be coached when Naismith didn't. He had his own ideas about rules and he'd go a long way to make a point. I remember Doc thought there should be a 10-second center line to eliminate stalling. We played Missouri and they led 4-2. It was our ball but we stayed under our basket. They stayed under their basket. Four of our players sat down and one stood with the ball on hip. Four of their players sat and one stayed up in case the guy with the ball went to the basket. The next year, there was a 10-second rule.

Doc didn't get everything he wanted with the rules, but he usually was heard. I respected him and everything he did for basketball. There's never been another one like him. I loved playing all sports, especially basketball, and playing for Doc made it that much more enjoyable.

THE PHOG ALLEN YEARS

Forrest Allen could be all things as the situation dictated. At the desk of his small Robinson Gymnasium office or at a Rotary Club luncheon, he would play the part of an administrator, a successful businessman or an executive. But in the basketball arena, he was transformed into a motivator — a coach preoccupied with the fundamentals of the game or an opinionated critic of those he felt didn't act in its best interests.

Every new season under Allen
began with a team meeting (left)
in a Robinson classroom where he
outlined the basics of the game.
This was always followed by the
showing of a movie clip of a cobra

and a mongoose, highlighting the elements of quickness, surprise and cunning.

All of Allen's home games were played in Hoch Auditorium —

most before sellout crowds of 3,800 fans. Then — just as they continue to do today — students lined up at the door 24 hours in advance to get seats for big games. During the championship

season of 1952, Bob Kenney (above) drives for a lay-up as the Jayhawks move through the Big Seven season and into tournament play.

The national championship, won in Seattle, was built around All-American Clyde Lovellette, but it included a supporting cast just right for the game as it was played in 1952. With victory assured in the championship game against St. John's, Allen took out Lovellette for the coach's usual reward, a fond handshake. The next day, as the team boarded the plane for its flight home, student manager Wayne Lauderback hand-carried the trophy and Chancellor Franklin D. Murphy beamed.

The team that Allen took to Seattle to win the championship (left) paid rapt attention in the locker room before the title game. One face stands out: Dean Smith, who would later carve out

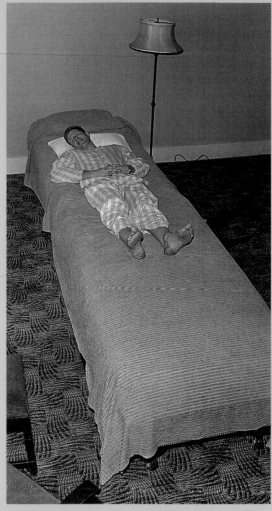

his own coaching history, sat at the center of the bench that night in Washington's Edmundson Pavilion. The hotel pulled two beds together (above right) for the 6-foot-9 Lovellette and the Kelley brothers from McCune (above), Dean and Al, studied for classes upon their return. The taping of Bill Lienhard's ankles (right) was done by longtime KU trainer Dean Nesmith.

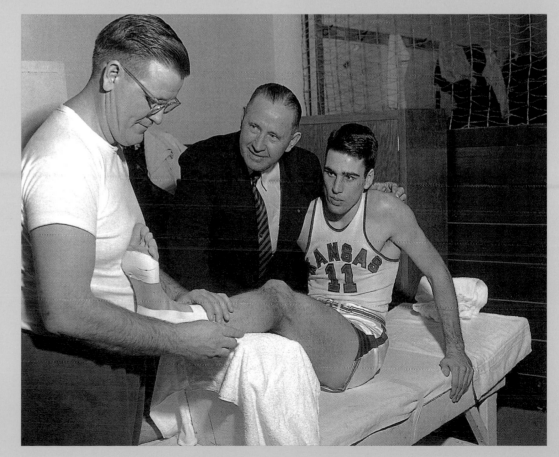

Trying to repeat the national championship in 1953 produced an epic game as Indiana faced the Jayhawks and a home crowd in Kansas City. With B. H. Born (bottom left) at center and Gil Reich (middle left) and Al Kelley (right) driving for baskets, the defending champions scrambled to the wire. Indiana coach Branch McCracken and Dr. Allen argued the fine points of timekeeping (above) as the game wound down to the final seconds. The final was 69-68, and Kansas settled for second.

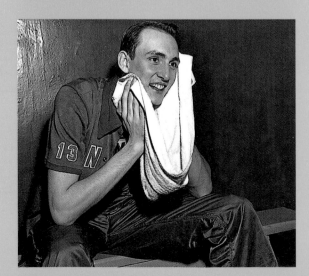

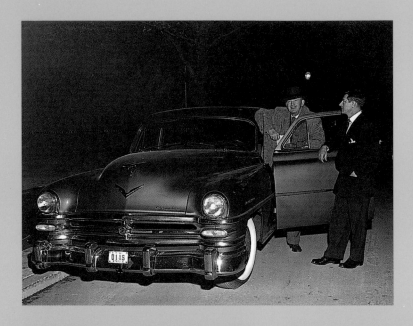

Phog Allen was outspoken, living the moment to its best, always dapper whether in his office, accepting awards or receiving an entourage of his former players in retirement. One of three cars presented him toward the end of his career was enjoyed by Missouri coach Sparky Stalcup. And always, Lawrence businessman Frank McDonald presided at each occasion in the Eldridge Hotel ballroom. Allen loved all these moments, but particularly the reunion of the 1952 team in the living room of his Louisiana Street house.

WILT AND A NEW GAME

BY BILL MAYER

The Phog Allen coaching tenure at Kansas ended under a cloud of contentiousness after the 1955-56 basketball season. An impossible task faced two men trying to help KU make the transition to another era that would be at least semicomparable to what Allen had accomplished in 39 seasons.

Wilt Chamberlain — even before he had played a single minute with the Jayhawks — was heralded as the greatest basketball player of all time. Dick Harp, the second key figure in the transition scenario, was a former KU star and an eight-year Allen assistant for whom there were painfully unrealistic expectations and pressures.

Both men left Mount Oread earlier than anticipated, both in frustration over their inability to do things the way they had hoped.

The 7-2, 275-pound Chamberlain, even more publicized than brilliant contemporaries such as Bill Russell and Oscar Robertson, shattered records, established himself as a phenomenal athlete, and in many ways enjoyed his college experience, far away from his urban homeland of Philadelphia. But he ultimately felt stifled and confined by the academic atmosphere and Midlands social climate and the clogging three- and four-man defenses thrown at him. Money also was a huge factor, because he loved to live well, relished female companionship,

and liked to drive good cars at near-supersonic speeds. A legal college scholarship did not lend itself to such a lifestyle.

Too, Wilt, at the tender age of 19, and Kansas had fallen a point short of North Carolina (54-53) in triple overtime in the NCAA title game of 1957. The Jayhawks, with Wilt missing two games due to illness, didn't even win their conference championship in 1958. An impatient Chamberlain did not envision the prospects for 1958-59 as being as good as they had been his sophomore season and embarked on a "show me the money" track.

After his Kansas junior season of 1957-58, The Big Dipper, the name he preferred over Wilt the Stilt, got a reported $10,000 from *Look Magazine* for rights to the story about why he was leaving the Jayhawks. Then he got a reported $50,000 to tour a year with the Harlem Globetrotters. At the time, National Basketball Association rules prevented Wilt from jumping straight to the Philadelphia professional team that had staked territorial claim to him after he finished at Overbrook High School.

Wilt's professional career, including a 100-point game and two NBA titles, requires several volumes, at least, to do it full justice. As of mid-1997, at age 60, he still held 58 NBA records, including one season with a whopping 50.1-point scoring average. He left Kansas having averaged 29.9 points and 18.3 rebounds over two years. Shot blocks were not tabulated and celebrated then as they are now, which was unfortunate because Wilt was a phenomenal shot blocker.

Still, Wilt left Kansas feeling unfulfilled and, whatever the reasons, has seldom been back to the area or the KU campus despite his being welcome and asked often. His jersey, No. 13, is waiting to be hung with others of distinction in storied Allen

Fieldhouse. But until he chooses to return for the "unveiling" ceremony, as have others with shirts in the rafters, No. 13 will remain undisplayed, in a drawer somewhere.

Whatever the conflicts, controversies and problems, the feeling is that the presence of Chamberlain in Lawrence for three years was an overwhelming blessing to Kansas basketball and added greatly to the Jayhawk heritage.

As the coaching successor to Hall of Famer Phog Allen, Harp faced the basketball equivalent of following Knute Rockne at Notre Dame and Bud Wilkinson at Oklahoma. In addition, Harp was inheriting the touted Chamberlain. How could Harp lose? Then there was an undercurrent of the "Phog no-retirement" thing. The inimitable Allen, who died in 1974 at age 88, was around the entire Chamberlain-Harp period and that didn't ease the changeover. All things considered, there was no way either Harp or Chamberlain could be inarguably successful.

A Kansas City, Kans., native with great athletic versatility, Harp's greatest dream as a youngster had been just to *letter* at Kansas. Dick wound up as a Jayhawk mainstay, a ferocious competitor who with the late Don Ebling co-captained the 1940 Kansas team that was beaten in the NCAA title game by Branch McCracken's Indiana Hoosiers. After World War II Army service and two years as William Jewell head coach, Harp became Allen's right-hand man at Kansas in the fall of 1948 and helped recruit key members of the 1952 college championship club.

Harp is one of the few men ever to both play and serve as a head coach in NCAA Final Four environments (1940 and 1957).

There are those who contend Harp was "too nice a guy … the perfect assistant but not tough enough as a head man." Some critics jibed, "He had too many morals and scruples and got too personally involved with his kids to make it in the cut-throat big time."

There never has been any hint that he wasn't an outstanding basketball mind — as witness the fact former pupil Dean Smith long sought and eventually hired Harp as an assistant down the line (1986-89). Others contend that considering the impossible task Harp was handed, he did about the best job anyone could have in similar circumstances.

Few have any idea of the innumerable problems Harp encountered trying to work the sophisti-

cated, streetwise, headstrong Chamberlain into a fabric that was best for Wilt, the team and the university.

Bob Billings, a Jayhawk player who is now a successful entrepreneur-developer in Lawrence, is highly complimentary of both Chamberlain, his college roommate, and Harp, for whom Billings played three years as a guard.

"You have to understand the tremendous pressures that both men had to cope with," Billings says. "Harp had to deal with promises for this and that and alumni expectations, hostility from pro-Phog Allen people who had wanted Phog to stay and coach Wilt and a rapidly changing sports picture that was increasing the emphasis on 'win at any cost.' People forget that Wilt was an 18-year-old kid when he came here. He was sophisticated, street-wise, bright and canny, and probably 15 years more mature than a lot of guys like I was from little Russell, Kans. People had been trying to take advantage of him when he first began to grow and excel as an athlete, and he was a good judge of who could and couldn't be trusted.

"But he still was only *18 years old*, uprooted and thrust into a less sophisticated Midlands environment far different from the inner-city experiences of his youth. Compared to what he was accustomed to in the East, it was a foreign environment, often leaving him with nothing he really wanted to do or enjoyed. He missed the social life from back home, yet he gave it a great effort in college.

"To his everlasting credit, Wilt really tried to make it work at Kansas while still maintaining some semblance of a personal life, considering all the attention he was getting — even when the media frenzy was a far cry from what it would be now. He loved social life and spent a lot of time in Kansas City, Topeka, Denver, Chicago, occasionally back in Philadelphia … where he had a number of friends. He went to class, tried to work with the team and wasn't always asking for special privileges. I spent a lot of time with the guy, roomed with him, love him dearly, and admire what he has been able to do under often adverse conditions."

Adds Billings: "Dick Harp, too, has often been misunderstood because he was not the gushy, outgoing type, and he was introspective, hard to get to know. But he has done so much for so many people and has been a truly great influence on basketball, not just at Kansas but everywhere. Neither Harp

The fieldhouse was full as the Chamberlain-led team huddled at the edge of the then-raised court.

"ONE THING I LEARNED QUICKLY ABOUT WILT. HE WAS SUPREMELY INTELLIGENT, LOYAL TO FRIENDS AND WHEN HE BECAME MOTIVATED ABOUT SOMETHING, ALMOST NOBODY OR NOTHING COULD STOP HIM . . ."

nor Wilt is likely ever to get the full credit he deserves for what he did and when he did it where KU basketball history is concerned."

Harp had a tendency to go far beyond coaching to make sure his athletes were getting along well, be it in sports, academics or social action. He was far ahead of his time in working with and assisting minority athletes and dealing with their special problems. At one point he was discussing a particular challenge with then-Kansas chancellor Franklin Murphy, and Murphy commented: "But Dick, why don't you leave *something* for the parents to do?"

Allen Fieldhouse was usually filled during the Chamberlain years, but attendance dropped off later after Harp was unable to win as consistently as many fans expected. Harp resigned under pressure in favor of then-aide Ted Owens after a 13-12 record in the 1963-64 season to take over an executive post with the Fellowship of Christian Athletes. His mark as Kansas head coach was 121-82 (.596).

While Harp did not meet the expectations of others on the job at KU, the person he disappointed most was himself. He was frustrated at not being able to work more miracles at a school he had dreamed of playing for and coaching at.

★ ★ ★

Recruiting in the Big Six-Seven Conference took a sharp turn for the competitive after World War II when Jack Gardner went from the Navy to Kansas State College and began to bring in topflight performers such as Howie Shannon. At Kansas, Allen often had been able to make contact with youths and then simply wait for players, like Harp, Howard Engleman, Ray Evans, Charlie Black, Ralph Miller and Otto Schnellbacher to show up, with some alumni help, of course. Those days were over.

After Allen had been injured in practice in 1947, he took a brief hiatus in favor of interim coach Engleman. Phog came back determined to win the national title and take the Jayhawks to the Olympic Games. He told Harp, then his neophyte assistant, in the fall of 1948 to turn heaven and earth to recruit the likes of Bob Kenney of Winfield, Bill Hougland of Beloit and Bill Lienhard of Newton. Meanwhile, Allen also put pinpoint focus on signing 6-9, 240-pound Clyde Lovellette, the superstar from Terre Haute, Ind.

The Allen-Harp combo got them all, and there was 1952 NCAA and Olympic glory (seven Jayhawks on the U.S. team).

Then came the flap over Chamberlain.

Upon being told that Chamberlain had decided to come to Kansas, Allen wryly commented: "Wonderful! I certainly hope he comes out for basketball." Later, Allen unknowingly put tremendous pressure on successor Harp by remarking that with Chamberlain, two aggressive male cheerleaders and two athletic coeds, anyone could win the national title.

Rumors abounded, with opponents sparking many of them, about how many "illegal" deals Kansas had made to get The Big Dipper. Certainly some promises were made and never kept, perhaps another factor in Chamberlain's eventual disillusionment. Nothing about early under-the-table offers was ever proved, but Kansas did get nailed for help alumni gave Chamberlain in arranging for automobiles. Wilt arrived here in a car, steadily upgraded his transportation and departed in a long, red Olds-mobile convertible that *Look Magazine* helped to finance. He admits he has always regretted he never got to play under Phog Allen, something he might have been promised during the recruiting process.

★ ★ ★

Allen Fieldhouse was dedicated in March of 1955 and it was a banner evening as Kansas upset Kansas State 77-67 to help honor Phog, in his next-to-last year as head man. But intense as that atmosphere was, it was rivaled on November 18, 1955, Phog's 70th birthday, when Harp's freshman team featuring Chamberlain met Allen's varsity and won 81-71, one of the rare times any KU frosh unit had ever prevailed.

The fieldhouse was a popular place that night, and Chamberlain didn't disappoint with his 42 points and 29 rebounds and an uncounted number of blocks.

If Chamberlain's freshman debut had been glossy, so was his eruption as a sophomore the night of December 3, 1956, against Northwestern.

The afternoon of the game, the *Lawrence Journal-World* ran a full-length shot of Chamberlain, about three feet off the floor, dunking a basketball. The awesome shot by photographer Bill Snead was two columns wide and ran the full depth of the front page. Northwestern players at the Eldridge Hotel, seeing the photo in the afternoon edition, were joking that it had been staged, with Chamberlain jumping off a chair as he jammed. They wouln't believe anyone could soar that high above the rim.

That night, Chamberlain exploded with 52 points (still a school record) and 31 rebounds. (Wilt's school record is 36.) Again, blocked shots were never chronicled, a shame because Wilt had so many. So the Chamberlain-Harp era began with an 87-69 romp past the Evanston Wildcats, later a top 10 team all season.

With Chamberlain on regular rampages, Kansas fell only to ball-stalling, keyhole-clogging Iowa State and Oklahoma State (both road games) and carried a 24-2 record into the NCAA finals in Kansas City against Frank McGuire's unbeaten North Carolina Tar Heels. It was a fierce, classic struggle that helped put college basketball on the big-time map for good. Television was just beginning to emerge, and the game was on the small screen across much of the nation. Joe Quigg's two free throws won the 54-53 triple-overtime classic after Kansas appeared to have the game won. A last-ditch effort failed to get the ball to the heavily defended Chamberlain.

Longtime Kansas observers think that game

was the undoing of both Chamberlain and coach Harp, branding them as "losers," unable to win the big one. Some feel the bad taste from the unfavorable aftermath of that game is a big reason why Wilt avoids coming back to KU.

The 1957-58 season for Chamberlain was also bittersweet. The Jayhawks wound up 18-5, not good enough for a league title or an NCAA appearance. Chamberlain missed playing in two of the losses. Kansas State was the league representative in the NCAA, and that feat by the archrival added salt in the wounds of Kansas fans.

As an all-around athlete, Chamberlain was phenomenal. In track he was a high jumper, long jumper and hop-step-jumper, and his strength was fantastic. A fierce competitor, Wilt was working with weights long before that trend had become ingrained in basketball at any level.

On Feruary. 28, 1958, Chamberlain scored something like 30 points and nabbed numerous rebounds in a 60-59 Friday night squeaker against Oklahoma in Lawrence. The next night at the league indoor track meet in Kansas City, with a bare minimum of workout time due to basketball, Chamberlain high-jumped 6-6³/4 to tie for the championship for the Jayhawks.

There had been rumors during his sophomore year that Chamberlain was not happy at Kansas and might quit, or transfer to a school in the East. The talk grew during his junior season and, in the final analysis, few — coach Harp included — were the least bit surprised with Chamberlain's decision to hit show biz with the Globetrotters.

The racial situation in Lawrence and the area was another factor in Chamberlain's leaving. Chamberlain noted that Kansas already had played black performers such as Lavannes Squires and Maurice King and perhaps thought there were no major problems. But he encountered discrimination in Kansas, in movies, barber shops, taverns, some restaurants and the like, and it turned his stomach.

How do you judge the Wilt era at KU?

"Wilt brought a lot to Kansas, and there was disappointment when he left, but his presence here was a great boost to basketball and for Kansas," Harp says. "Blessing or curse? Is that what you want to know about Wilt? He certainly was no curse. There were times when you had to wonder if it was all blessing. But I think he benefited from coming to KU and we benefited in many ways from his being here."

Chamberlain seemed to opponents to be more than one player.

THE WILT CHAMBERLAIN AND DICK HARP YEARS

PHOTOGRAPHS BY RICH CLARKSON

Two events made the 1956-57 season a pivotal year for Kansas basketball: Wilt Chamberlain was now a varsity player and Dr. Allen had retired. Wilt scored 52 points in his first varsity game against Northwestern, adding to the expectations that he — and KU — would dominate college basketball. And questions swirled around new coach Dick Harp. Could he build a team around Chamberlain that would lead to another national championship? Could the popular former assistant successfully replace a coaching legend? Jayhawk basketball was a whole new game.

Chamberlain seemingly could do anything. His ability to rise above the basket with an unstoppable dunk was what everyone wanted to see, but Wilt could also shoot from the outside, even a finger roll, and that dazzled all. Always surprising the fans, he entered the high jump of the Kansas Relays,

finishing second with a jump of seven feet, all without doffing his ever-present cap. And when the locker room food selections were inadequate at the Big Eight Tournament, Wilt stopped by the concession stand in Kansas City's Municipal Auditorium to buy ice cream.

Dick Harp is one of only five men to both play and coach in an NCAA Final Four championship game. He was the starting guard on the 1940 Kansas team that lost to Indiana in the finals. He began his coaching career at William Jewell College in Liberty, Mo. Dr. Allen brought Harp back to Lawrence as his assistant in 1944 and he became head coach in 1956. Popular with the press and respected by his players, he was the man on the hot seat as Chamberlain's coach.

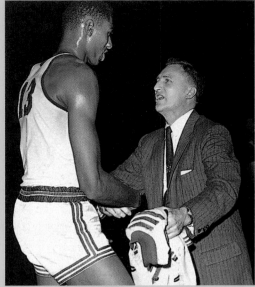

When aficionados of the game argue over the greatest NCAA title game ever played, 1957 always gets votes. Kansas arrived with Chamberlain, who scored 32 points to lead the Jayhawks past San Francisco 80-56 in one semifinal. North Carolina took three overtimes against Michigan State to get to the finals. The epic championship game took three overtimes to decide. Kansas and Chamberlain controlled the game early, but Carolina, playing with a team largely recruited from the New York area, came back. The tension was high as Harp took time for strategy for the overtime.

Kansas used a box and one defense to dog UNC star Lennie Rosenbluth. Carolina's strategy was a sagging defense around Chamberlain. Although Wilt played well and the Jayhawks were positioned to win the game in the final overtime, an errant pass missed Chamberlain and the game was over. Harp consoled Chamberlain as stunned cheerleaders looked on. But it was more likely that Harp needed the consoling. In the early '60s, Harp resigned to join the staff of the Fellowship of Christian Athletes.

THE AGONY, THE JOY

BY CHUCK WOODLING

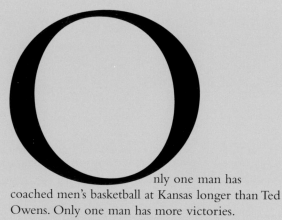

Only one man has coached men's basketball at Kansas longer than Ted Owens. Only one man has more victories.

Yet Owens's name is seldom, if ever, mentioned in the same sentence with the legendary Phog Allen.

Days after he was fired in 1983 following 19 seasons on Mount Oread and with 348 victories, Owens said: "Only history will determine what kind of job we did here . . ."

History has shown that Owens's nearly two decades at Kansas were more like KU football than KU basketball. Still, Owens coached many more winning seasons than losing ones — 14 winning, four losing and one .500.

Perhaps Owens's most notable distinction was his ability to survive back-to-back losing campaigns. He did that in the early '70s, compiling 11–15 and 8–18 records in the years after he had taken arguably his best team to the NCAA Final Four.

No doubt the freshness of that Final Four visit is all that kept Owens from the guillotine following the eight-win 1972-73 season — the worst for Kansas since the early days of the Depression.

Owens bounced back smartly the next year. Rejuvenated with a talented freshman in Norm Cook and a spirited junior college transfer in Roger Morningstar, the Jayhawks made an improbable journey to the Final Four in 1973-74.

And that, in effect, is pretty much Owens's career in microcosm — two losing seasons sandwiched between two Final Four berths.

Ted Owens came to Kansas in 1960. A former guard at Oklahoma known for his deadly two-handed set shot, Owens had been eminently successful during a four-year stint at Cameron A&M, a junior college in his native Oklahoma.

Dick Harp, the man who had succeeded Allen, brought Owens in as an assistant coach. Four years later, after Harp resigned, Owens became only the fifth head basketball coach in school history.

Many people — notably Allen's progeny — were shocked by the school's decision to promote Owens when Ralph Miller, a former KU All-American who had been highly successful at Wichita State, was available.

With that albatross around his neck, Owens launched his major-college career in 1964-65 with a 17-8 record, not good enough by current standards, certainly, but since it was the most victories by the Jayhawks in four years, the naysayers couldn't really complain.

Then Owens literally shut their mouths. Six of his next seven teams won 20 or more games, and three of those six were ranked among the top five in the wire service polls.

Walt Wesley, a gangly 6-11 center, and guard Jo Jo White, later an NBA standout with the Boston Celtics, were the ringleaders during back-to-back 23-4 seasons that silenced Owens's critics.

The 1965-66 team — Owens's second — may have been his best. That club went into the NCAA Tournament ranked No. 4 nationally, but lost to eventual national champion Texas Western (now Texas-El Paso) in the regionals. Kansas appeared to have won at the end of the second overtime when White sank a 35-footer from the corner. However, an official ruled

White had a foot on the out-of-bounds line. Texas Western won, 81-80.

Kansas came right back the next year to post another 23-4 season. It, too, ended in stunning fashion. Again the Jayhawks dropped a heartbreaker in the NCAA regional — 70-68 to Louisville. That defeat was doubly disappointing because it happened in Allen Fieldhouse.

During the next three seasons, Owens went into a gradual decline — 22-8 and a second-place finish in the NIT, 20-7 and a first-round loss in the NIT, and then 17-9.

Thus after a half-dozen years, Owens appeared to have come full circle with a 17-8 record in his first year and a 17-9 record in his sixth year.

Would the slide continue? Or would Owens find the "up" button again?

He found it, all right … and the "up" button was attached to a skyrocket.

Led by the inside play of 6-11 senior Dave Robisch and the outside shooting of 6-5 junior Bud Stallworth, the 1970-71 Jayhawks exploded onto the national scene and accomplished the rare feat of going undefeated in the Big Eight.

Kansas went to the Final Four in Houston with a 27-1 record. They came home from the Astrodome 27-3 after bowing to UCLA in the semifinals and to Western Kentucky in the third-place game.

Not that it mattered. Just going to the Final Four was enough to rekindle the enthusiasm. Owens was riding high. In his first seven seasons, Owens had compiled a 149-43 record. That's a .776 winning percentage, higher than any previous KU coach, including Allen, whose 39-season winning percentage was .729.

Those were halcyon days for Owens.

Nobody could know at the time, of course, but the next dozen years would be full of ups and downs. Owens, in fact, managed only three 20-plus victory seasons in his last 12 years.

Those three teams were:

• The 1973-74 team went 23-7 and to the Final Four in Greensboro, N.C. KU lost both games — to Marquette and UCLA.

• The 1977-78 team went 24-5, won the Big Eight championship and lost to UCLA in a first-round NCAA regional game. Too bad because this team — featuring Darnell Valentine, Paul Mokeski, John Douglas, Donnie Von Moore and Ken Koenigs

— may have been the deepest Owens ever had.

• The 1980-81 team went 24-8 and bowed to Wichita State in the NCAA regional semifinals.

Poor recruiting doomed Owens to losing seasons in 1981-82 (13-14) and in 1982-83 (13-16).

KU athletic director Monte Johnson had been on the job only four months when he pulled the plug on Owens on March 21, 1983, and hired Larry Brown to replace him.

Owens had finally run out of lives. His winning percentage had dipped from that glossy .776 in 1971 to .657.

When Owens bowed out, he stated that he believed his mediocre 1982-83 team "… has laid the foundation for greatness in Kansas basketball."

At the time, that comment sounded like so much coach-speak. Today we know Owens was a prophet.

The 1982-83 roster had two freshmen in Ron Kellogg and Calvin Thompson and a red-shirt in Greg Dreiling. They would later become three-fifths of the starting lineup on the winningest team in Kansas basketball history. Brown took that trio, added Danny Manning and Cedric Hunter, and fashioned a 35-4 record while earning KU's first trip to the Final Four since Owens's 1973-74 team.

And it wasn't just that Brown-coached 1985-86 team, either.

In the 14 years since Owens uttered that "laid the foundation" remark, Kansas has made 13 NCAA tournament trips, including four to the Final Four, won an NCAA title and compiled no fewer than 19 victories every season.

Those 14 consecutive years of post-Owens consistency are the antithesis of his 19 years on Mount Oread. In truth, the only thing consistent about Owens's tenure was its inconsistency.

Curiously, the man who had one job for 19 years has had numerous jobs since leaving Lawrence. Owens has been an investment broker and a TV analyst. He has been head coach at Oral Roberts University and of the Fresno Flames, a professional team that never played a game.

Owens has coached the Maccabai basketball team in Israel and scouted for the New Jersey Nets. He has also coached the boys basketball team at Metro Christian Academy in Tulsa, Okla.

Today, at age 68, he is athletic director at St. Leo, a small college near Tampa, Fla.

The obligatory handshake pat-on-the-back at the close of a Kansas-Kansas State game between Ted Owens and Jack Hartman, the Kansas State coach and friendly rival.

THE TED OWENS YEARS

PHOTOGRAPHS BY RICH CLARKSON

Intensity was the word that best expressed the atmosphere in Allen Fieldhouse during the Ted Owens years: intensity on the bench during the games; intensity during pregame admonishments to victory; intensity every day in practice. Although there were some disappointments, Owens's intensity often resulted in victories and memorable seasons.

Dave Robisch took the Jayhawks through the 1970–71 season undefeated in the Big Eight, to the Big Eight preseason tournament title (here in Kansas City's Municipal Auditorium), and to the Final Four. But in the national semifinals, KU ran into the UCLA juggernaut. Kansas lost to the Bruins 68–60.

The Jayhawks seemed to own Municipal Auditorium in the days of the preseason Big Eight tournament. Here, Pierre Russell scores to help the Jayhawks win the 1968 tournament championship, their fifth straight title. The holiday tournament, played between Christmas and New Year's, was replaced by the postseason tournament in 1979.

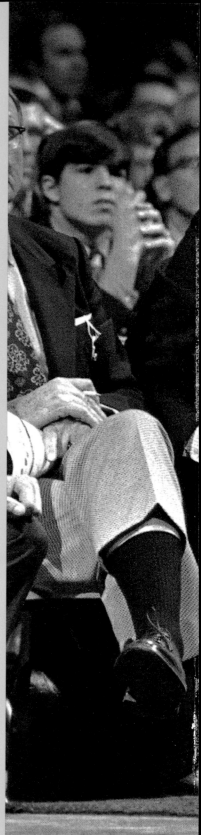

When the game began, Owens was on top of every move of his players — and the officials, by whom he was well-regarded. He became the second winningest coach in Kansas history (348 wins,182 losses) behind Allen and was named Big Eight Coach of the Year five times and National Coach of the Year in 1978.

Uncomfortable moments would come from time to time as Owens and assistant coaches Bob Frederick and Sam Miranda watched the games unfold. Each brought experience as a player to his coaching career: Frederick at Kansas, Miranda at Indiana and Owens at Oklahoma.

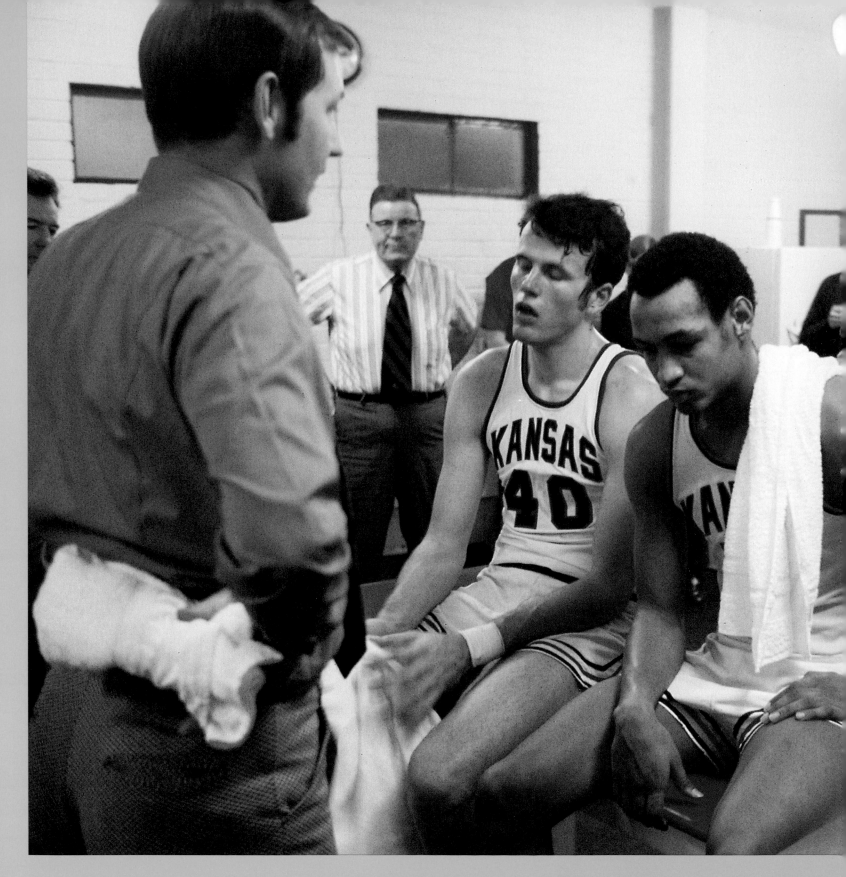

In the early '70s Owens led his team to two Final Four appearances. Players listened in the quiet of the locker room as their coach spoke. Owens served as assistant to Dick Harp and stepped up to the head coaching position when Harp resigned following the 1963-64 season.

Rodger Bohnenstiel joined with Jo Jo White on the 1965-66 and 1966-67 teams to win successive Big Eight titles. Both years the Jayhawks were ranked in the top four, only to lose in NCAA tournament play to eventual Final Four teams. Bohnenstiel ended his career with 1,006 points and was team scoring leader in 1967, when he was named All-Big Eight.

The Final Four was only fractions of an inch away in 1966 when Kansas played double overtime in the regional against eventual national champion Texas Western (now UTEP). With Kansas behind 81-80 and time running out, Jo Jo White took the pass on the sidelines and launched a 35-foot jumper that went in at the buzzer. Kansas fans rejoiced, but the celebration was short-lived. Official Rudy Marich made the call: Jo Jo's shoe was touching the out-of-bounds line.

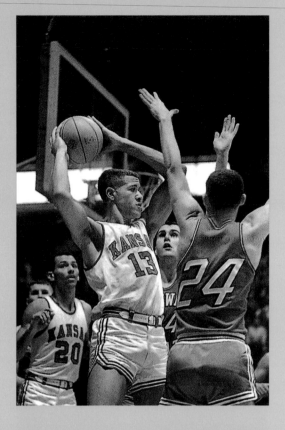

There were great moments and great players. All-Americans Bud Stallworth (far left, celebrating after he scored 50 points against Missouri in 1972 to set the conference single-game record), Walt Wesley (No. 13 above, who led the Jayhawks in scoring in 1965-66) and Darnell Valentine (lower left, who holds the record for most free throws) were leaders on their Jayhawk teams. Paul Mokeski (above) was a rebound leader who went on to a solid career in the NBA.

THAT CHAMPIONSHIP SEASON

BY CHUCK WOODLING

I f Phog Allen was the Jupiter of the Kansas University basketball galaxy, then Larry Brown was the Hale-Bopp Comet, a bright light in the sky that soon vanished into the firmament.

Anyone who coaches KU basketball for five years is regarded as a short-timer, but five years for Brown, a man who has never found a cure for itchy feet, was nearly an eternity.

Brown's legacy was the improbable NCAA championship in 1988. People still shake their heads. How did Brown do it? Whatever, Kansas went into the 1988 NCAA Tournament with a 21-11 record and a No. 6 seed. No team with as many as 11 defeats had ever won a national title, but Kansas won it all.

Sure, it was a fluke … but Brown's half-decade at Kansas wasn't. All five of his teams qualified for the NCAA Tournament and two of them went to the Final Four. His overall record was 135-44. That's a winning percentage of .754.

Notably, too, Brown's record in Allen Fieldhouse was 71-5. Brown lost two home games during his first season and three more during his last season and in between fashioned a 55-game home-court win streak, the longest in school history.

Through it all — five 20-plus win seasons and that long home-victory string — Kansas fans dealt with seemingly constant rumors about Brown leaving. There was other turmoil, too, like when Brown fired assistant coach Jo Jo White, a KU icon.

Brown had coached the New Jersey Nets for two years when he was hired as Ted Owens's replacement on April 8, 1983. Prior to that, Brown had spent two seasons at UCLA. Before that, he'd been with ABA and NBA teams.

At his introductory press conference on Mount Oread, Brown alluded to his vagabond tendencies and said: "I hope it stops. I hope I'm gonna be here a long time … hopefully a long, long time."

For the peripatetic Brown, five years *was* a long, long time.

Since leaving Kansas, Brown has spent three and a half years as head coach of the San Antonio Spurs, a year and a half with the L.A. Clippers and four years with the Indiana Pacers. Now he's in his first season with the Philadelphia 76ers, his sixth NBA team.

Clearly, Brown can't stay in one spot very long. Still, no one has ever impugned his coaching ability.

Brown's reputation as a teacher was borne out at Kansas when he took basically the same personnel that had finished 13-16 under Ted Owens and guided them to a 22-10 record in 1983-84. It helped to have seven-footer Greg Dreiling, who had red-shirted during Owens's last season, but Dreiling wasn't a franchise player.

Brown's meal ticket had arrived in Lawrence, though. Danny Manning was a senior at Lawrence High School, a 6-11 transfer from Greensboro, N.C. It wasn't a coincidence that Brown had added Ed Manning, Danny's father and a former NBA and ABA journeyman forward, to his coaching staff.

Young Manning, who would go on to become the most decorated basketball player in Kansas University's long and prestigious history, was the second-leading scorer (14.6) on a 26-8 club that stumbled by two points to Auburn in the second round of the NCAA Tournament.

Wait 'til next year. With all five starters returning, preseason pundits predicted a promising third season for Brown. Promising, indeed. Kansas went on to win 35 games — still a school record — and lose only four.

Nevertheless, that season ended bitterly when Duke dumped the Jayhawks, 71-67, in a Final Four semifinal. The loss left Brown to wonder if he would ever have another Kansas team as good as that one.

Manning and point guard Cedric Hunter would return for the 1986-87 season, but the eligibility of sweet-shooting wing men Ron Kellogg and Calvin Thompson and center Dreiling had expired. As it turned out, the drop-off wasn't drastic. Still, the Jayhawks had to rely too much on Manning and Hunter. Brown's fourth Kansas team had compiled a 25-11 record. All 11 defeats were on the road, including a decisive 70-57 loss to Georgetown in the third round of the NCAA Tournament.

Four years at Kansas . . . a long time for Brown to stay put. Would he return?

Finally, on May 7, 1987, Brown issued this statement: "I'm staying at the University of Kansas. It's final."

In deciding to remain at Kansas for a fifth season, Brown was buoyed by two factors: Bob Frederick, a friend, had been hired as the Jayhawks' new athletic director. And Manning would be back for his senior year.

Manning couldn't do it single-handedly, but Brown figured the addition of Marvin Branch, a 6-8 junior college transfer, would push the Jayhawks over the hump.

And so the season of destiny began.

Kansas dropped back-to-back games to Iowa and Illinois in the Maui Classic, then rang up seven straight victories before bowing to St. John's, 70-56, in New York City. Worse, the Jayhawks lost starting forward Archie Marshall to a season-ending knee injury in that defeat.

Still, with junior Milt Newton filling in for Marshall, the Jayhawks chalked up three straight wins before suffering another crushing blow. Branch was ruled academically ineligible for the second semester. Without Branch, Kansas lost five of six. Somehow, though, the Jayhawks captured nine of its last 12 to land an NCAA berth.

First stop on the road to the championship: Lincoln, Neb. The Jayhawks disposed of Xavier, 85-

72, then escaped with a 61-58 victory over Murray State. On to the Pontiac Silverdome where they socked Vanderbilt, 77-64, then eliminated Kansas State 71-58, the team that had ended the 55-game home-court winning streak a month earlier.

Kansas City, here they came — Kemper Arena, site of the 50th Final Four.

In the semifinals, Kansas erupted for a big early lead against Duke and hung on for a 66-59 victory.

Finally, thanks mainly to a 31-point, 18-rebound performance from Manning in his last college game, the Jayhawks avenged two regular-season losses to Oklahoma by turning the Sooner Schooner into a pumpkin, 83-79.

Cinderella wore crimson and blue. Meanwhile, Brown was seeing blue and gold sugarplums.

Less than a week after the championship game, Brown told UCLA he was coming back.

Then Brown changed his mind overnight.

"After thinking about it, I've decided to stay at the University of Kansas," Brown said.

A couple of months later, his motives became moot. He was gone again, this time for good. In mid-June, the San Antonio Spurs lured him back to the NBA.

Curiously, a week after Brown accepted the Spurs' post, Kansas officials received a letter of inquiry from the NCAA relating to improprieties in the men's basketball program.

About four months later, the punishment was announced. Kansas would be the first school in NCAA history prevented from defending its championship because of rules violations. The infractions, according to the NCAA, were related to providing illegal benefits — mostly to a potential transfer from Memphis State named Vincent Askew — during a 10-month period while Brown was coach.

Later, Brown would angrily say of the NCAA probation: "I'm not ashamed of anything we did. I'm proud of what we did at Kansas."

Brown's fleeting five years were sprinkled with turbulence and tainted by probation, but in the pantheon of Kansas basketball he will always be remembered first and foremost as the man who coached "Danny and the Miracles" to the 1988 NCAA championship.

Ray Meyer, the DePaul coach, visited with Brown the day before their game in NCAA play.

LARRY BROWN YEARS

PHOTOGRAPHS BY RICH CLARKSON

Larry Brown arrived on Mount Oread in 1983, recommended by Dean Smith and signed up by athletic director Monte Johnson. Brown took a team with none of his own recruits to a Big Eight post-season title and a winning record in his first year. It began a new era of Jayhawk basketball — a winning one.

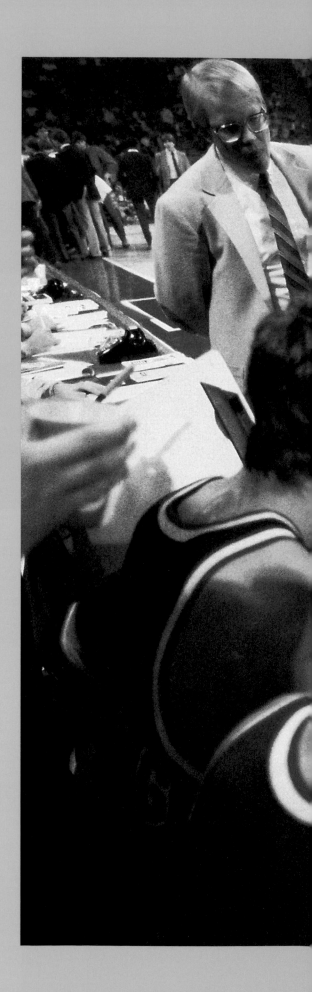

Danny Manning became the most decorated basketball player in Kansas annals, finishing his career with 31 points and 18 rebounds to lead the Jayhawks to their 1988 national championship. Playing Oklahoma for the third time that season, the Jayhawks won 83–79 in the Final Four's 50th anniversary game in Kansas City's Kemper Area. The Jayhawks lost 11 times that year, but somehow found a way to get to the national semifinal game, which featured a matchup of point guards Kevin Pritchard and Duke's Quin Snyder. But the real contest came Monday night when Manning was unstoppable in the second half.

While at Kansas, Brown captivated the fans, the student body and his teams with a mixture of unique drive and sincerity. Assistants Bob Hill and Ed Manning (Danny's father) would follow him to the NBA. An eventual NCAA probation along with Brown's surprising resignation left Kansas fans and officials puzzled at best, bitter at worst. But while it lasted, Brown could coach and motivate his Jayhawk teams to accomplish miracles, and the ride for all was a heady one.

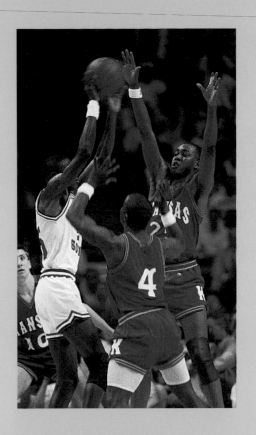

With Manning dominating play in Kansas City, the NCAA trophy headed for Lawrence and Brown headed for San Antonio. But for the team that celebrated the championship, the story of Danny and the Miracles will be retold many times in future years.

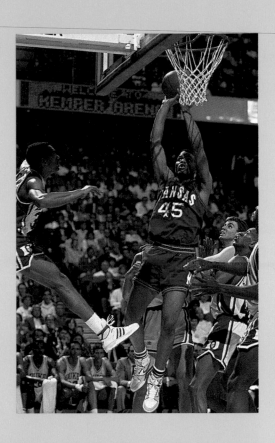

Brown's habits became
legendary in Lawrence and
included mandatory conditioning runs for the coaching staff
across the Lawrence countryside.
There, assistants Bob Hill, John
Calipari and Ed Manning huffed
and puffed to keep up with him
each day. And the days began
early at Carol Lee's Doughnuts
on West 23rd Street, Brown's
morning haunt.

In 1940, Charlie Black posed
looking to make the Allenesque pass.

Milton Allen, Phog's youngest son, also
posed as his father would approve.

PICTURE DAYS

The first day of basketball practice in the fall
has traditionally been picture day, when the group
picture and all the individual photos of the players
and coaches are taken. In recent years, this has
turned into media day, and there are more television cameras and interviews than still pictures
being shot.

For many of the early years, the principal
photographer was Duke D'Ambra whose storefront shop next to the
Dickinson Theater on Massachusetts was the origin of most of the
published pictures from KU sports.

Duke often would cover KU games and put the prints on a
train to Kansas City or New York where newspapers would publish
them days later. Duke charged $1 to take each picture. Never one to
waste either time or film, Duke often took only one picture, always
followed by the rejoinder, "Goodbye!" With that, he would pick up
his tripod and camera and move on.

As the years went by, the "posed action" picture came into
vogue. Players would be asked to drive, shoot, pass and guard for
pictures. Those pictures were furnished to newspapers and
magazines by the sports information office. Then newspapers began sending their own photographers to picture
days. Competing for unusual angles and peak action, the
photographers arrived with more and more ideas, cameras and stepladders. And picture day became a full-
fledged workout for the players.

Paul Endacott (far left) posed in the studio when he was named "Helms
Foundation Player of the Year" in 1923. Years later on picture day, KU's
legendary sports information director, Don Pierce, demonstrated to
players how to drive to the basket, though his playing days were as an all-
conference football lineman.

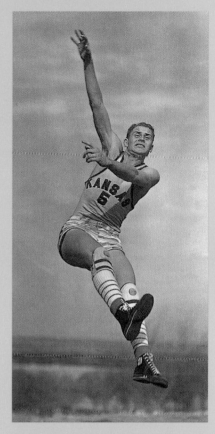

Howard Engleman was photographed leaping high from the crest of Mount Oread.

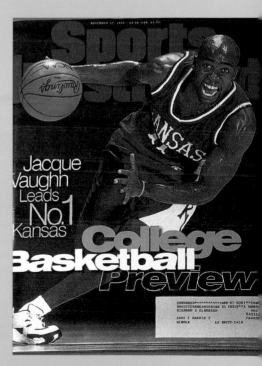

Wilt Chamberlain, tying his shoes, was selected by *Sports Illustrated* as one of the magazine's most-memorable portraits.

Jacque Vaughn cut and drove for *Sports Illustrated's* cover.

The *Lawrence Journal-World's* Bill Mayer interviews Dr. Allen as fans wait patiently.

Max Falkenstein, always the voice, shared the microphone once with Lovellette.

Writers Jay Simon (left), Dick Snider of *The Topeka Daily Capital* and Bob Busby of *The Kansas City Star* covered Kansas in the '50s and '60s.

THE REPORTERS

The early days of basketball reporting at KU are in marked contrast to today's television satellite trucks and reporters' laptop computers.

Then, the sportswriter pulled each sheet out of his typewriter and handed it to a Western Union agent who transmitted the story back to the writer's newspaper. For years, Skipper Patrick of the Associated Press, Bob Busby of *The Kansas City Times*, Jay Simon of *The Topeka State Journal* and Dick Snider and Bob Hentzen of *The Topeka Daily Capital* were the regulars along with Bill Mayer and Harry Morrow of the *Lawrence Daily Journal-World*. Bob Nelson reportedly delayed his graduation for years to cover the Jayhawks for the student newspaper, the *University Daily Kansan*.

Kansas City's first television station, WDAF-TV, was the first to broadcast a Kansas game from Hoch Auditorium. And for years, WREN in Lawrence and Topeka, with Max Falkenstein at the microphone, was the principal play-by-play source for Jayhawk basketball.

Don Pierce was KU's first full-time sports information director. He turned out game programs, press releases, and the seating chart for the writers' row and answered the media questions, all single-handedly.

When KU began its own radio network, the Voice of the Jayhawks over the years included many sportscasters who went on to the networks, including Tom Hedrick, Merle Harmon, Bill Grigsby, Monte Moore, Gary Bender, Kevin Harlan and Bob Davis.

And always, Max Falkenstein was at courtside.

Photographer Duke D'Ambra was as much a KU fixture as the new campanile.

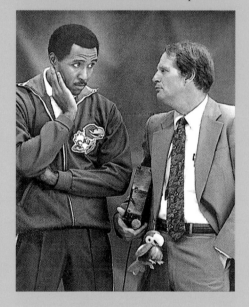

Tom Hedrick (with tape recorder and Jayhawk doll) was the voice in the '60s.

Topeka sports editor Bob Hentzen records the words of Jacque Vaughn.

THE CONTRIBUTORS

ALEXANDER WOLFF is a senior writer for *Sports Illustrated* whose first love is college basketball, As such, he has covered 14 Final Fours, visited all the major basketball schools in America, and spent many days in both Lawrence and Chapel Hill. He played in the noontime game in Allen Fieldhouse with Matt Doherty, Bud Stallworth, and Sean Pearson. In that game, he guarded Calvin Rayford which he says resulted in severe whiplash.

CHUCK WOODLING is a native Nebraskan who gave up Big Red football for Crimson and Blue basketball when he became sports editor of *The Lawrence Journal-World* in 1969. He has followed Jayhawk basketball teams across the country and was the author of *Against All Odds*, the book chronicling KU's 1988 national championship.

DAVID HALBERSTAM, the Pulitzer Prize-winning author, loves basketball and once spent an entire season with the Portland Trailblazers for the book *The Breaks of the Game*. His books include *The Best and the Brightest*, *The Powers That Be* and *The Reconing*.

JOE POSNANSKI, a columnist for *The Kansas City Star*, has frequently covered Kansas basketball since his arrival in Kansas City in 1996. Prior to that, he was a sportswriter for *The Charlotte Observer* and columnist for *The Augusta Chronicle* and *The Cincinnati Post*.

BILL MAYER, the one-time sports editor and later managing editor of *The Lawrence Daily Journal-World,* is now retired but still writes a regular column reminiscing about great times atop Mount Oread.

TED O'LEARY was an All-America starting guard for the Jayhawks from 1928 to 1932. After moving through a variety of journalistic posts, he settled in as the regional correspondent and regular writer for *Sports Illustrated* in Kansas City, where he also reviewed books for *The Kansas City Star.*

JOHN McLENDON JR. is retired in Cleveland after a lifetime of coaching basketball. A member of the Naismith Memorial Hall of Fame, he is the author of two books, *Fast Break Basketball* and *The Fast Break Game.*

ACKNOWLEDGMENTS

Of the many people who helped make this book possible, those at the University of Kansas include Dr. Robert Frederick, the athletic director, and members of the staff including Richard Konzem, Doug Vance, Dean Buchan and Susan Wachter. A special thanks goes to Roy Williams for unusual access and hospitality; to assistant coaches Matt Dougherty, Neil Dougherty, Joe Holiday and Ben Miller, and trainer Mark Cairns. Behind the scenes are the student managers headed in 1997 by Jill Johansen and including Stephanie Temple, Olivia Thompson, Joel Zuniga, Blake Flickner and Damon Miller.

Kansas City Star sportswriter Blair Kerkhoff, author of the 1996 book *Phog Allen, The Father of Basketball Coaching,* was a great team player in assisting Ted O' Leary, whose fingers no longer dance across the keyboard as they once did. Blair helped commit Ted's tales to paper.

Two KU graduates provided additional pictures: Bill Frakes on assignment for *Sports Illustrated* for part of the 1996-97 season and Earl Richardson photographing every game for *The Lawrence Journal-World.* And that newspaper's deputy editor, Bill Snead, an unusually talented photographer as well as editor, has been an adviser, contributor and friend for many years. Ned Kehde of the Spencer Research Library provided wonderful early pictures.

And from past years, the role of many individuals contributed to the impetus, the background and the special feel for the rich tradition of Kansas basketball. They certainly included such amazing individuals as Dick Harp, Don Pierce and Jay Simon as well as the many fellow journalists including those who wrote here along with Dick Snider, Bob Hurt, Bob Hentzen, Pete Goering, Jeff Jacobsen and Bob Nelson. In addition to Dr. Allen and Harp, coaches Larry Brown and Ted Owens were generous with help and friendship in addition to invitations to photograph even the inner sanctums of their teams.

Over those years, a number of opponent coaches extended unique friendship and help to one of "those Jayhawks," including Sparky Stalcup and Norm Stewart, Tex Winter and Jack Hartman, Bob Knight and Henry Iba.

ADDITIONAL PHOTO CREDITS

Duke D'Ambra, pages 6-7, 11, 13, 140 (3), 141 (upper right)
Earl Richardson, pages 8-9, 29
Jeff Jacobsen, page 71
Bill Frakes, *SI*, pages 10, 18, 20-21, 50
Peter Read Miller, *SI*, Page 141 (lower right)
Vogt Studio, page 140 (lower left)
Lawrence Journal-World, page 115
University of Kansas archives, pages 6-7, 78-79, 80, 87

AFTERWORD

Growing up in Lawrence, Kans., at the end of World War II, it was inevitable that I would run headlong into basketball. But my first real encounter was almost by accident. One afternoon not long after an adventurous group of us kids discovered the steam tunnels under "the hill," we surfaced in Robinson Gymnasium. Our group had been exploring the underground of the KU campus, seeing what buildings each doorway from the tunnels would reveal.

Thus, we emerged in Robinson, and, boys being boys, we explored up the stairway only to find ourselves watching the Jayhawk varsity team practicing. So we sat on the floor at the end of the gymnasium for a moment. As the practice came to our end of the floor, the coach whom we all recognized as Phog Allen walked over to introduce us to the gentleman in the tweed suit sitting nearby.

That is how I happened to meet Dr. James Naismith.

You couldn't grow up in Lawrence without KU basketball, and it was a few short years later in high school when I picked up my first camera that basketball became the principal subject of my pictures. By my senior year in high school, I was "freelancing" KU basketball games for *The Lawrence Journal-World, The Kansas City Star, The Topeka Daily Capital,* the Associated Press and Acme Telephoto.

I would photograph the first half of the games in Hoch Auditorium, race for my darkroom, process the first-half pictures and rush to catch the Kansas City and Topeka buses with the picture packages. Then, I would get back to Hoch for the final minutes of the game and more pictures. Then to the Dine-A-Mite.

When I was a freshman at KU and working part-time for the *Journal-World,* I volunteered to pay my way to cover the road trips of the team, both photographing the game and writing the story for the newspaper. Thus, I traveled with Dr. Allen's blessing, accompanying the team for the out-of-town games until my senior year. Dr. Allen, ever the absent-minded professor, would arrive at season's end having misplaced many of the receipts and records. With the accounting for the season in financial disarray (though within budget), the task of calculating my share was difficult. Thus, each summer, Dr. Allen would congratulate me on the pictures and excuse the expenses.

On those trips, I was included as a team member (in fact, I would have various travel roommates from Wayne Lauderback, the student manager, to a substitute from Topeka by the name of Dean Smith) and would even eat the pregame meals of honey, toast and hot tea. On more than one occasion, Dr. Allen would get me on the training table to straighten out my sacroiliac, which was always responsible for whatever was ailing me at the time including the common cold.

When Wilt Chamberlain arrived in Lawrence shortly after the dedication of Allen Fieldhouse, KU was clearly big time. Thus, I naively dropped into the mail my first posed action and portrait pictures from the picture day, all to that new magazine, *Sports Illustrated.* My pictures arrived on the desk of the picture editor, Jerry Astor, the morning the magazine decided to do a Chamberlain story that week and they used a portrait of Wilt tying his shoes. Later in Chamberlain's first varsity season, Astor called to give me my first assignment for the magazine: to photograph Wilt playing against Iowa State and Gary Thompson for a small story at the back of the magazine.

Only at the last minute, the Crosby golf tournament was rained out on the Monterey Peninsula and the Chamberlain-Thompson story became an eight-page lead story. That was the point when I became an *SI* regular that took me to many Kansas games in addition to all those I photographed for *The Lawrence Journal-World* and for some 20 years, *The Topeka Capital-Journal.*

Even after moving from Kansas, the pull of KU basketball has brought me back to Lawrence many times and even this past year, traveling with and being part of a Roy Williams entourage, it all seemed very natural. The players change, the coaches change and some Lawrence landmarks change. But Allen doesn't and tradition doesn't.

Kansas basketball was home again.

—Rich Clarkson
Denver, August 1997

In the end, all Kansas fans — none more than the cheerleaders — go sky-high for their Jayhawks.

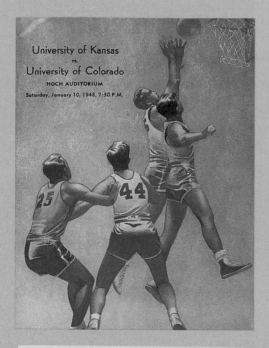

University of Kansas
vs.
University of Colorado
HOCH AUDITORIUM
Saturday, January 10, 1948, 7:30 P.M.

Kansas University . . . . . St. Joseph's
U. of South. California . . . . Temple

CONVENTION HALL   DECEMBER 30, 1942

PHILADELPHIA   — OFFICIAL PROGRAM 15 CENTS

BASKETBALL
Kansas U. vs. Missouri U.

Score:

Kansas U.

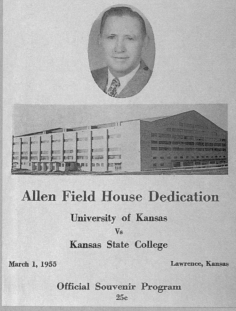

Allen Field House Dedication

University of Kansas
Vs
Kansas State College

March 1, 1955   Lawrence, Kansas

Official Souvenir Program
25c

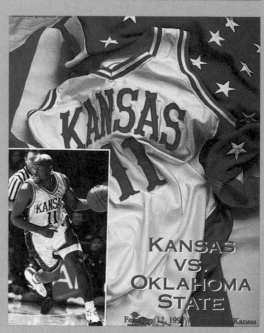

KANSAS
VS.
OKLAHOMA
STATE

KANSAS
★
OKLAHOMA

TUESDAY
March 1, 1960
ALLEN FIELD HOUSE,
LAWRENCE

NEXT HOME GAME
NEBRASKA
MONDAY, MARCH 7

KANSAS

10c   SAINT LOUIS

MONDAY
DECEMBER 4, 1961
ALLEN FIELD HOUSE
LAWRENCE

NEXT HOME GAME
KANSAS ★ SAINT JOHNS
K. STATE ★ MARQUETTE
FRIDAY, DECEMBER 15

KANSAS
★
KANSAS STATE

SATURDAY
March 11, 1967
ALLEN FIELD HOUSE
LAWRENCE

25c

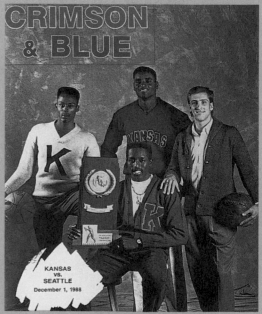

CRIMSON
& BLUE

KANSAS
VS.
SEATTLE
December 1, 1988